Voices of Africa

Edited by
Barbara Nolen

Etienne Tamwelah

TAMO FREDRICK
B.P. 4 NUM

Fontana / Collins

First published by Charles Scribner's Sons
(as *Africa is Thunder and Wonder*) 1972
First issued in Fontana Books 1974
Second Impression January 1975

Copyright © 1972 Barbara Nolen Strong

Made and printed in Great Britain by
William Collins Sons & Co Ltd Glasgow

CONDITIONS OF SALE:
This book is sold subject to the condition that it shall not, by way of trade or otherwise, be lent, re-sold, hired out or otherwise circulated without the publisher's prior consent in any form of binding or cover other than that in which it is published and without a similar condition including this condition being imposed on the subsequent purchaser

Contents

Africa *Langston Hughes*	9
Introduction	11
Prayer to Masks *Léopold Sédar Senghor*	17

Part I: The World of Spirits

My Mother Was a Witch *D. O. Fagunwa and Wole Soyinka*	21
The Fetish Child *Samuel Asare Konadu*	25
HAUSA TALES *translated by H. A. S. Johnston*	
The Man with the Ugly Wife	33
The Severed Head	34
Chief Sekoto Holds Court *Bessie Head*	36
How a Devil Danced to Death *A. Doris Banks Henries*	41
The Television-handed Ghostess *Amos Tutuola*	43
I See a Lonely Dead *Prince Modupe*	47
IMAGES OF DEATH	56
The God of War *from the Yoruba Tribe*	56
The Sorrow of Kodio *from the Baulé Tribe*	57
Death *from the Kuba Tribe*	58

Part II: Village Voices

Kenya Our Motherland *John Mbiti*	60
SONS OF AFRICA	61
Coming of Age *John S. Kado*	61
Out of Disaster *R. Lucy Kuria*	63
Exile *Alhaji Sir Abubakar Tafawa Balewa*	64
The Old Man of Usumbura and His Misery *Taban Lo Liyong*	72
Tekayo *Grace Ogot*	78
Chief Priest of Ulu *Chinua Achebe*	90
The Geography Lesson *Mongo Beti*	94
My Husband's Tongue Is Bitter *Okot P'Bitek*	101
The Untilled Field *Joseph Waiguru*	105

THREE SOUSSOU TALES	109
The Sweetest Thing	109
The Moon	110
The Well	110
The Winner *Barbara Kimenye*	110
The Epic of Liyongo *Muhammed Kijuma*	121
Africa's Plea *Roland Tombekai Dempster*	128

Acknowledgments

Grateful acknowledgment is made to the following copyright holders for permission to reprint the poems and stories indicated below:

AFRICA by Langston Hughes. From *Selected Poems of Langston Hughes*. Alfred A. Knopf, Inc.

PRAYER TO MASKS by Léopold Sédar Senghor. From *Selected Poems*, by Léopold Sédar Senghor, translated and introduced by John Reed and Clive Wake. Copyright © Oxford University Press, 1964; reprinted by permission of Atheneum Publishers, New York.

MY MOTHER WAS A WITCH by D. O. Fagunwa. From *The Forest of a Thousand Daemons*, translated by Wole Soyinka. Thomas Nelson & Sons Ltd., London, 1968.

THE FETISH CHILD by Samuel Asare Konadu. From *A Woman in Her Prime*, by Samuel Asare Konadu. Heinemann Educational Books Ltd., London, 1967.

THE MAN WITH THE UGLY WIFE and THE SEVERED HEAD. From *A Selection of Hausa Stories*, compiled and translated by H. A. S. Johnston. Oxford at the Clarendon Press, London, 1966.

CHIEF SEKOTO HOLDS COURT by Bessie Head. From *When Rain Clouds Gather*, by Bessie Head, reprinted by permission of Bessie Head and Victor Gollancz.

HOW A DEVIL DANCED TO DEATH by A. Doris Banks Henries. From *Liberian Folklore*, by A. Doris Banks Henries. Macmillan & Co. Ltd., London, Basingstoke, and Canada, 1966.

THE TELEVISION-HANDED GHOSTESS by Amos Tutuola. From *My Life in the Bush of Ghosts*. Reprinted by permission of Faber and Faber Ltd., London, 1954.

I SEE A LONELY DEAD by Prince Modupe. From *I Was a Savage*, by Prince Modupe. Copyright © by Prince Modupe. Reprinted by permission of Paul R. Reynolds Inc., New York.

THE GOD OF WAR. From *African Poetry*, edited by Ulli Beier. Cambridge University Press, London, 1966.

THE SORROW OF KODIO, translated by Miriam Koshland and recorded by Leon G. Damas. Copyright © 1959 by the Atlantic Monthly Company, Boston, Mass. Reprinted with permission.

DEATH. From *African Poetry*, edited by Ulli Beier. Cambridge University Press, London, 1966; reprinted by permission of *Jeune Afrique*, Press Africaine Associée, Paris.

KENYA OUR MOTHERLAND by John Mbiti. From *Drum Beat*, chosen by Lennard Okola. East African Publishing House, Nairobi, 1967.

COMING OF AGE by John S. Kado. From *When I Awoke*. East African Publishing House, Nairobi, 1966.

OUT OF DISASTER by R. Lucy Kuria. From *When I Awoke*. East African Publishing House, Nairobi, 1966.

EXILE by Alhaji Sir Abubakar Tafawa Balewa. From *Shaihu Umar*, by Alhaji Sir Abubakar Tafawa Balewa. Longmans, Green & Co. Ltd., London, 1967.

THE OLD MAN OF USUMBURA AND HIS MISERY by Taban Lo Liyong. From *Fixions and Other Stories*, by Taban Lo Liyong. Heinemann Educational Books Ltd., London, 1969.

TEKAYO by Grace Ogot. From *Land Without Thunder*, by Grace Ogot. East African Publishing House, Nairobi, 1968.

CHIEF PRIEST OF ULU by Chinua Achebe. From *Arrow of God*, by Chinua Achebe. Copyright © 1964 by Chinua Achebe. Reprinted by permission of William Heinemann Ltd., and Bolt & Watson Ltd.

THE GEOGRAPHY LESSON by Mongo Beti. From *Mission to Kala*, by Mongo Beti. Heinemann Educational Books Ltd., London, 1958; reprinted by permission of Rosica Colin Ltd.

MY HUSBAND'S TONGUE IS BITTER by Okot p'Bitek. From *Song of Lawino*, by Okot p'Bitek. East African Publishing House, Nairobi, 1966.

THE UNTILLED FIELD by Joseph Waiguru. From *Origin East Africa*, edited by David Cook. Heinemann Educational Books Ltd., London, 1965.

THE SWEETEST THING, THE MOON, and THE WELL. From *Three Soussou Tales (Etudes Guineenes)*, edited by Ezekiel Mphahlele and Ulli Beier. Longmans of Nigeria Ltd., 1947.

THE WINNER by Barbara Kimenye. From *Kalasanda*, by Barbara Kimenye. Oxford University Press in Three Crowns Books, London, 1965.

THE EPIC OF LIYONGO by Muhammed Kijuma. From *Swahili Poetry*, by Lyndon Harries. Oxford at the Clarendon Press, London, 1962.

AFRICA'S PLEA by Roland Tombekai Dempster. From *Poems of Black Africa*, edited by Langston Hughes. Indiana University Press, Bloomington, 1969.

Every effort has been made to locate all persons having any rights or interests in the material published here. If some acknowledgments have not been made, their omission is unintentional and is regretted.

Africa

Africa
Sleepy giant
You've been resting awhile
Now I see the thunder
and the lightning
In your smile
Now I see the storm clouds
In your waking eyes:
The thunder
The wonder
And the new surprise
Your every step reveals
The new stride
In your thighs
        Langston Hughes

Introduction

I have been called home to Africa on consultations, and thus have read this anthology in the air, on land, and on the beach. Perhaps it is fitting that I should write this introduction here in Africa, surrounded by the silent mountains, the blue sea, and the flaming hibiscus flowers.

The many voices that make up the African scene must be understood because of the increasingly important role that Africa is now playing in world affairs. A most useful introduction to the mind of the modern African can be found in his literature, which has been greatly stimulated by the surge of national independence sweeping over the continent. The great opportunities for self-government and self-expression have gone hand-in-hand and are amply reflected in the wide variety of imaginative and realistic writing included in this anthology.

Most African writers have a European language as their second language. There are a few exceptions, such as writers from some parts of Senegal, Gambia, Sierra Leone, Liberia, and South Africa. The majority of African writers from the former British colonial empire use English. Those in the former French and Belgian colonial territories, such as Senegal, Ivory Coast, and Congo-Kinshasa, have French as their second language. African writers from Angola, Mozambique, and Guinea-Bissau similarly use Portuguese.

Africa itself has many languages. In any one African country alone there may be many vernacular languages. Sierra Leone, for example, officially an English-speaking territory, has a population of three million, among whom there are fourteen languages, with Temne, Mende, and Limba being dominant. People from the different language communities speak or write to each other in the language of the European power of which they were once colonies. Thus the European language is not only a medium of expression to the outside world, as in this anthology, but it is also an internal unifying force for each nation. It may be argued that a second language learned at school cannot be used with sufficient conviction and skill. It should be remembered, however, that great writers of English prose like Arthur Koestler, and before him, Joseph Conrad, were not originally English-speaking. The mastery of European languages by Africans is another evidence of their adaptability to world currents of scholarship and literature.

Literature in African languages as such does exist and is found particularly with large language groups like North African Arabic, Swahili in East Africa, Hausa, Yoruba, and Twi in West Africa, and Zulu in South Africa. Some of it has been translated into English and French.

There is a great deal of imagination and style in African writing and this is displayed against the background of the experience of an individual, his community, his nation, and his race. These exotic qualities give African literature a flavour which is both attractive and educative.

Several arrangements are possible in the collection of any continent's literature. In African anthologies, classification has been often made into regions or by literary form in which the division is usually into poetry, articles, and novels. Barbara Nolen has chosen an unusual framework which hovers between the spirit world and the setting of urban modern Africa. Sometimes these two intermingle; at other times they separate; but throughout, the wonder that is remains evident.

Almost all the writers are established ones who have been writing for some years. The original publication may not be easily available, however, and it is very much to the credit of the anthologist that she has been able to bring them together in such a powerful form by grouping them under separate and significant umbrellas.

But the poems scattered throughout the book are all-embracing. Individually they provide the answer to one question, that of the famous black poet Countee Cullen, 'What is Africa to me?'

Inevitably, in the poems there is a confrontation between

white and black in Africa. This confrontation originated long ago with exploration and continued with legitimate trade, and, later, the illicit slave trade, missionary endeavour, military conquest, subjugation, and finally, both colonialism and white and brown colonization. There was an implicit assumption that European civilization was better for the black man than his own African variety. But even in a country like Liberia, which has had over a century of contact and some assimilation with Europe and the United States, the poet still protested and insisted on his cultural identity. (I quote throughout the introduction from poems reprinted in their entirety in the text.

> God made me *me*.
> He made you *you*.
> For God's sake
> Let me be *me*.
>   *Dempster*

The loss of liberty which colonialism brought to many Africans and all its griefs and humiliations are lightly passed over now in the present era of independent Africa. But the grave acts of racial injustice still remaining in South Africa, Rhodesia, and the Portuguese territories are constant reminders of the past and are like probes worrying a newly healed wound. The African has learned to comfort himself. He has to comfort himself in order to free his mind and attention for the greater task of nation-building.

For this, however, like all other nations and peoples, he needs to draw strength from a heroic past, the existence of which has always been denied him because others who had exploited him wished to justify and ease their consciences by doing so. We know from firm historical evidence that such an Africa existed. That Africa, which the poet Léopold Sédar Senghor, President of the Republic of Senegal, has seen in the silent masks distilling the 'air of eternity' in which he breathed the air of his ancestors. . . .

The physical beauty of Africa shines through this anthology from the west of the continent to the snow-capped peaks of

Mount Kenya and Mount Kilimanjaro in the east.

In a symbolic way the poets meet and join with Mother Africa, facing the future:

> We are the men of the dance, whose feet draw
>   new strength pounding the hardened earth.
>
> *Senghor*

> Sand dunes roll over eternal silence
> Tomorrow's cure for strained nerves.
>
> *Mbiti*

Together the poems cover the scope of the anthology, outlining as it does the varied aspects of the world of spirits, the voices of the village, the people of the city, and the African personality.

More particularly, the section on 'The World of Spirits' illustrates the mythology and religion of Africa, in a vivid way bringing to light the subjective emotions which are described in scientific detail in many works of social anthropology. This is a world peopled by demons and witches and images of death, made evident to human beings, and in some cases matched by man, especially when the latter is endowed with extra cunning or supernatural powers, as is the case with twins.

Yet even the supernatural must make some concessions to modernity. The suspected witch to be condemned to death is saved by a medical postmortem report; the ghostess has a magical television set in her hand. Another witch is unable to escape death from the bullets of a gun – although in death only her damaged skull changes back to human form, the remainder, even post-mortem, retaining the form of the antelope into which she usually changed for her predatory excursions. These are folktales half-believed and half in the form of the European Grimm-Andersen-Kafka tradition. They are most often told in villages in a small circle in the evening, under the starlit sky.

These villages in Africa and their busy, lively inhabitants crisscross in the next part of the anthology. Some are Moslems, some Christian, and some pagan. Some clearly are of the nineteenth century, as that written about in the excerpt from the book of the late Abubakar Tafawa Balewa, first Prime Minister of Nigeria. But, in others, the round mud hut has given way to the oblong house. Telegrams announcing the winning of football pools bring about the appearance of hordes of relations, and the reader finds himself firmly in the twentieth century even though he is still inside the African countryside.

For the African personality is many-sided, and this anthology shows the response of the African to the challenge of independence, to that of grappling successfully with a new world, and to that of fighting prejudices of race, sex, and colour.

In African literature, the crackle of lightning of past memories gives a vivid flash of the African landscape before we hear the long roar of thunder; and then all is silence. But the wonder will always remain.

Africa, 1971   ABIOSEH NICOL

Prayer to Masks

by Léopold Sédar Senghor

Masks! Masks!
Black mask red mask, you white-and-black masks
Masks of the four points from which the Spirit blows
In silence I salute you!
Nor you the least, Lion-headed Ancestor
You guard this place forbidden to all laughter of women, to all smiles that fade
You distil this air of eternity in which I breathe the air of my Fathers.
Masks of unmasked faces, stripped of the marks of illness and the lines of age
You who have fashioned this portrait, this my face bent over the altar of white paper
In your own image, hear me!
The Africa of the empires is dying, see, the agony of a pitiful princess
And Europe too where we joined by the navel.
Fix your unchanging eyes upon your children, who are given orders
Who give away their lives like the poor their last clothes.
Let us report present at the rebirth of the World
Like the yeast which white flour needs.
For who would teach rhythm to a dead world of machines and guns?
Who would give the cry of joy to wake the dead and the bereaved at dawn?
Say, who would give back the memory of life to the man whose hopes are smashed?
They call us men of coffee cotton oil
They call us men of death.
We are the men of the dance, whose feet draw new strength pounding the hardened earth.

Part 1

The World of Spirits

We do not really mean, we do not really mean,
that what we are going to say is true.
Ashanti storyteller

My Mother was a Witch

by D. O. Fagunwa
and Wole Soyinka

Wole Soyinka is the translator and Chief D. O. Fagunwa is the author of this tale of the African world of spirits, in which it seems perfectly natural for a young man to say, 'My mother was a witch.' Both author and translator are Nigerians of the Yoruba tribe.

Wole Soyinka, born in Nigeria in 1935, is a poet, playwright, and novelist. He is best known as a playwright, however, and seven of his plays have been produced with distinction in England and Africa. No less gifted a writer could have translated the sound and action of Yoruba storytelling so sensitively into modern English.

The Forest of a Thousand Daemons, from which this selection is taken, is the first work of the late Chief Fagunwa to be translated into English. It is also his most famous novel. Four other novels in the Yoruba language have been read and enjoyed by thousands. Their vivid language and vigorous action are typical of one aspect of Yoruba literature, and at the same time they are essentially African.

My name is Akara-ogun, Compound-of-Spells, one of the formidable hunters of a bygone age. My own father was a hunter, he was also a great one for medicines and spells. He had a thousand powder gourdlets, eight hundred *ato*, and his amulets numbered six hundred. Two hundred and sixty incubi lived in that house and the birds of divination were without number. It was the spirits who guarded the house when he was away, and no one dared enter that house when my father was absent – it was unthinkable. But deep as he was in the art of the supernatural, he was no match for my mother, for she was a deep-seasoned witch from the cauldron of hell.

Once my father had nine children, of whom I was the eldest; four wives and my mother was the most senior of them. She had four children, the wife who was next to her had three, the next two and the fourth had none at all. One day my mother and another of these wives had a quarrel and took the case to my father for settlement. He found my mother at fault and this so angered her that she resolved to take vengeance for the slight. She became so ruthless in her witching, that, before the year was out, eight of my father's children were dead and three of his wives had gone the same way. Thus was I left the only child and my mother the only wife.

Look on me, my friend, and if you are not yet married I implore you to consider the matter well before you do. True, your wife ought to be beautiful lest you tire of each other quickly; and a lack of brains is not to be recommended since you must needs hold converse with each other, but this is not the heart of the matter. The important requisite is that your wife should not be prone to evil, for it is your wife who gives you meat and gives you drink and is admitted most to your secrets. God has created them such close creatures that there hardly exists any manner in which they cannot come at a man; and when I tell you what my father suffered at the hands of this wife of his, you will be truly terrified.

It happened one day that my father prepared himself and set off to hunt. After he had hunted a long while, he felt somewhat tired and sat on a tree stump to rest. He was not long seated when, happening to look up, he saw the ground in front of him begin to split and smoke pour upwards from the rent. In a moment the smoke had filled the entire area where my father sat so thickly that he could not see a thing; all about him had turned impenetrably black. Even as he began to seek a way of escape he observed that the smoke had begun to fuse together in one spot and, before he could so much as blink, it fused completely and a stocky being emerged sword in hand and came towards my father. My father took to his heels instantly but the man called on him to stop and began to address him thus:

'Can you not see that I am not of the human race? I arrived even today from the vault of the heavens and it was on your account that I am come hither, my purpose being to kill you. Run where you will this day; kill you I most resolutely will.'

When he had spoken thus, my father was truly afraid but even so he steeled his heart like a man and said, 'Truly, as I observe you, I know you are not of this world, and I see also that the sword in your hand spells mortal danger for me. Nevertheless, I implore you, and I charge you in the name of the immortal God, do not fail to tell me the nature of my offence.'

The man replied to him, saying, 'Do you not know that you have grievously offended your Maker? That you have ruined his handiwork even to this extent, that you sent eleven souls to heaven when it was not yet the hour allotted them by their God?'

These words of his were a great astonishment to my father, for while it was true that he was well versed in magic and charms, he did no one any evil. So he replied to him, 'If this is indeed your complaint then your mission is to a different man; it certainly is not I. Since the day I was born I have never harmed anyone: I do not see a man going about his business and take umbrage at his existence; I do not see a rich man and suffer thereby from envy. When I see a man at his dinner I continue on my own way. I have never inflicted wounds on any man, I have not shot a man down in my life, so how can you claim my life, and for a crime of which I am innocent!'

He waited for my father to finish his speech and then he replied, 'True, you have not with your own hand killed anyone, but you have been responsible for the suffering of poor innocents. With your eyes wide open to what you did you married a deep-dyed witch for the mere beauty of her body – is that an act of goodness? Does the blood of your many wives not call out to you? Does the crime against your eight children not hang round your neck? And, despite all of this, do you have the gall to tell me that you have never been guilty of evil? Indeed there is no remedy;

kill you I must.'

Only then did my father call to mind the kind of woman he had taken to wife, and so he replied to him, 'Truly I see now that I have sinned. I have a wife whom I cannot control, I strut like a husband merely in name. What I should have done I have left undone, the path I should have trodden I have neglected, the creature who deserved to die at my hand I have indulged with praises. Ah, stranger from the dome of heaven, forgive me.'

When he heard this, the man forgave my father and desisted from killing him, but he warned him that he must, the moment he returned home, put my mother to death. So saying, he turned into the forest and continued his travels that way.

When he had gone my father took up his gun and returned home. And it so happened that the path he took led him past a field of okro on the way to the town. It was evening when he came there, the moon was already up, and, coming up to the field he looked over to the other side and observed someone approaching from that direction. Quickly he climbed up a tree, waiting to see what this person was about. The figure came on unswerving until it vanished into a large anthill. Shortly afterwards, an antelope emerged from this anthill, entered the field and began to feed on the okro. My father brought his gun to bear on the creature and drove furnaces into its skull. The gun had no sooner roared than there came from the antelope a human cry and the words, 'Ah, woe is me!'

That night my father slept in a little hut by the field. When daylight broke he went to the spot where the antelope was shot, but he found nothing there, only blood. He began to follow the trail of blood, and it was with increasing astonishment that he found that the trail led homewards. He followed it until he arrived right home. But in midtown the trail vanished completely and he did not come upon it again until he was nearly at his own doorstep: then it led him straight into my mother's room.

I had not myself slept at home that night. Whenever my father was away I hated to spend the night at home because the spirits gave one no peace all through the night. Even my mother rarely slept at home and then only when my father gave his permission. I returned to the house just as my father was opening the door to my mother's room, and when he had opened the door and we entered, that moment when I caught sight of my mother, it was all I could do not to take flight. From her head down to her shoulders was human enough, but the rest of her was wholly antelope. She was all covered in blood and swarms of flies. My father touched her; she was dead and had begun to rot. Indeed she was the antelope stealing out at night to feast in the field of okro.

And so did my mother die, and hardly was a month over when my father also followed her. From that day was I orphaned, fatherless and motherless. And thus ends the story of my parents.

From The Forest of a Thousand Daemons, *by D. O. Fagunwa, translated by Wole Soyinka, Thomas Nelson & Sons Ltd., 1968.*

The Fetish Child

by Samuel Asare Konadu

Samuel Asare Konadu is a member of the Ashanti tribe in central Ghana. Born in 1932, he was educated in local schools and served an apprenticeship in journalism and broadcasting in what was then the Gold Coast. He received a scholarship to study journalism in Europe and, on returning to Ghana, he began his writing career, basing his work on research into the traditional life of his people. Eight of his novels and a number of his short stories have been published, many of which deal with the African belief in the supernatural.

Pokuwaa, the heroine of his novel *A Woman in Her Prime*, from which the following selection is taken, is a mature, sensitive woman who has been married three times without bearing a child. In desperation and hope, she plans to sacrifice at the shrine of the great god Tano. If the god is pleased with her, she will bear a fetish child, as children in her village are called when they are born with the help of a god or goddess.

Today was Friday and the day of sacrifice for the great god Tano.

Pokuwaa returned home from her last trip to the river and went quickly into the kitchen to place the water there ready for use. Daybreak was near and her excitement was mounting. She ran through the compound to the bathroom outside her hut, bumping into the bamboo enclosure in her haste. She stripped off her clothes and scooped the water over her body. The water was a bit chilly in the morning air. She should have heated it, she thought, 'but if it saves me a little bit of time . . .' Time at Brenhoma was counted by the sun and now although the sun was still behind the clouds, very soon it would break out and the shadows could lengthen. Speeding up, she slipped on the stone floor and had to step into the wooden water container to steady herself.

Very soon the house of Tano would begin to fill with people, and she had to hurry to get there in time for her turn at consultation and sacrifice. She could feel inside her the drums that would sound for the gathering for sacrifice in all the neighbourhood. People would bring yams, sheep, goats, eggs, cowries. What a person had to sacrifice depended on her requirements. In some cases people were asked to bring cows.

Pokuwaa thought how lucky it was for her that it had to be simply a hen and eggs; though it had been difficult getting a hen that was black all over.

She dashed back to her room, rubbed her limbs with some shea cream; then she sprayed herself with smooth white clay powder. This was for purification and it was essential on this day of sacrifice. That done, she hurried out of her room with her calabash full of eggs.

Where was the black hen? Pokuwaa went to the post where the hen had been tied and at sight of the broken string, her mouth fell open. She began to tremble. Who could have given that string a twist and broken it? She rushed outside and began searching under the small bushes there.

'What evil spirit wants to spoil the day for me?' she moaned. 'Help me, O Almighty. Help me.'

She ran into her room to get some more grain. With this she started off to look for the hen in the village. If she could see it, she would spread the corn to lure it back to her.

For three days she had kept watch over the black hen and today, the day of the sacrifice, the hen was missing. It had been difficult to obtain such a hen in the vicinity of her own village, Brenhoma, and she had had to travel over six miles to buy one from the next village, Nsutem. The owner had insisted on taking two hundred cowries for it. Pokuwaa had tried to bargain for one hundred and sixty, and the owner, who knew the value of that black hen, had refused. These jet-black hens were always being sought after, and if this buyer didn't buy it, another was bound to come along some day. Someone else would be quite willing to pay two hundred cowries.

So Pokuwaa had paid and taken the hen to Brenhoma, put a single bead on its leg for identification and tied it up for safety. And now the hen was gone.

'But it was there this morning,' she remembered. 'I spread some corn for it.' She looked round again.

' "Eat well, this might be your last feed," I said to the hen as I spread the corn. And it pecked eagerly and swallowed the lot before I could leave the house to collect another pot of water from the river. I went into the room with the waterpots, picked up the last pot and came out to find that it had already finished all the corn. I said, "You need more. You must eat to keep alive. I need your blood." I put down my pot, went back inside, scooped another handful of grain and spread it for the hen before I left the house.'

Further than this she could not remember. Had the hen been there when she returned from the half-mile walk to the river? She couldn't remember. On her way down to the river she had been busy with her prayerful thoughts, beseeching her ancestors and the gods to bless her efforts to get a child. She had prayed to God:

'You are not an unforgiving God,
God of our forefathers.
Your assistance is not temporary.
You are almighty.
Let all evil men fall before you.'

The importance of this Fofie, this festive Friday which came once every six weeks, had crowded her mind. This day, gods and goddesses moved among men to feast and grant people's requests. And they were powerful. They could answer her need for a child. The ancestors of her father and mother would surely help her. If she herself had wronged anyone or if the sins of her parents or ancestors were being avenged on her, the deities could be besought to spare her the pain of not having a child of her own. That was why she had been told to get the black hen. Jet black, that was it. Was the black hen not there when she returned from this last trip to the river?

What had happened in fact was quite simple: as soon as Pokuwaa had gone out of the house a cock had come along and joined in the feast. Then he had started making approaches to the hen. It was not easy in the game with a string round the hen's legs and so in the struggle that followed the string made of old raffia palm had snapped. The hen, now freed, had followed the cock out of the shed, and out of the yard. The hen had taken a dust bath, and then the two of them had ventured out into a narrow lane leading to the bush outside the village.

Pokuwaa rushed along at first, but, seeing no sign of the black hen, she slowed down to look more closely in nooks and corners among the crowding huts.

Soon she came upon some children playing in a lane. 'Children,' she pleaded, 'have you seen a black hen here?' One of them started to run away. 'Why,' she called, 'come back! I want you to help me find my black hen.'

One of the children soon volunteered an explanation. 'He is running away because he has been throwing stones at a black hen which passed . . .'

'What?' interrupted Pokuwaa eagerly.

'. . . at a black hen which passed here a few minutes ago. That is why he is running away,' he continued.

'Show me where you saw the hen,' said Pokuwaa, controlling herself.

'There!' many eager mouths shouted; and many hands pointed towards the bush outside the village.

'Where? Come with me and show me.' Pokuwaa now addressed herself to the little boy who was said to have been throwing stones at the hen. He looked younger than his seven years, and had bushy hair with cowries and shells tied on it.

Pokuwaa looked at this boy and felt immediate sympathy for him. She knew that such children should not be harshly treated, let alone beaten. For it was feared that if they were beaten the fetish would take them away. And so they were pampered and especially cared for.

'Take me where you threw stones at the hen,' entreated Pokuwaa, reaching for the hand of the fetish child.

The other children trooped after them. Soon they reached a mango tree.

'That was where I first saw the hen. It was with a group of fowls, but it cackled the loudest, and I threw a branch. I just threw a branch,' he rattled on. 'And it went over there.'

Pokuwaa was now getting impatient. She looked at the rising sun in the crimson sky, and knew that if she was to get to Tano's home in time, she would have to hurry. It was with an effort that she reminded herself that she mustn't get cross with a fetish child. It was one such child that she herself was seeking – and if she was successful . . .

'Oh, God,' she groaned, 'who could have set that hen free? Who?'

They were almost at the bush outside the village, and there was nothing to do but to enter it and search there also. By now she was really worried.

Could this perhaps be the work of evil spirits who, knowing Tano's greatness, had spirited the hen away, to stop her from making her sacrifice? She knew, at least she had been told, of ghosts who walked the streets at night, of fiery witches who stayed on tree-tops doing all kinds of wickedness. They had power to turn things into small objects and, through incantations, spirit them away. She had been told of a child who had been turned into a chicken and slaughtered; of a man who had turned himself into a crocodile and devoured a young girl who had jilted him.

'But here I am,' Pokuwaa thought aloud, 'taking the words of Tano seriously. And now I can't find the black hen.' It had been on a Friday six weeks ago that, in the unlit room of Tano's shrine, the oracles had told her to bring this black hen and eggs to be offered to the spirits so that they might bring her *madwowa* back to her. She had sacrificed four times before; white cloth, and cowries in tens, without any success; but this time the demand for sacrifice had come from Tano himself, and Tano was great.

'Great Tano,' she cried, 'assist me in my plight. You are powerful and nobody can thwart your will.'

Would she find this hen in time, or was this day to be lost to her even if she did find it – if she found it too late?

'What a world. When you find the hoe you can't find the stick. When you find the stick you can't find the hoe. Oh, Adwoa Pokuwaa! I am in a tight lane.' She was weeping now, seized with the fear that if she failed to make the sacrifice and lost this chance of bearing a child, her fate as a barren woman would be made certain. Then her old age would be doomed to loneliness; no child to care for her, no grandchildren to warm her compound and no issue of her blood at all to mourn at her death. She would be buried of course by the relatives and her brothers' children would be there, but there was nothing better than having your own children at your funeral.

The children with her had turned the search into a game of hide-and-seek. Some went behind bushes, throwing pebbles at each other and imitating bird and animal sounds. Others were giving chase. Only the fetish child continued to search with Pokuwaa.

They were getting into denser bush when her eyes fell on a shiny black back, through a tangle of thorny stems. Her heart leaped and she thrust her arm through the thorns without caution. Her hand was stabbed, but as she withdrew it what she noticed more than the pain was the blood that dripped on to the green leaves at her feet. She was fascinated by the red of her blood, and a thought ran through her that with this red fire in her, this fine blood, she was certainly young enough to have a child.

Why was the hen so still? Was it dead? The noise from the children should be enough to startle it if it was not dead. And yet dead hens always lay on their back or on their side, never on their belly. If this turned out to be a hen indeed, and alive, and with a single bead on its foot, then her day was saved.

She broke off a branch and began to push the thorns aside to make an opening, and before she knew it the fetish child had shot through to the other side and was making his way towards that black back in the bushes beyond. There could be no mistaking that cackling. It was a hen. But why was the fetish child pulling? They both saw at once. They saw the black snake that had been trying to swallow the hen.

Then everything happened at once. The fetish child shot back in fear; the children screamed and ran away; and Pokuwaa tore her way through the thorns towards the black hen and the black snake. She wasn't afraid of snakes. She had killed one at an early age and had lost her fear of them long since. Soon the black snake was flattened out on the ground and she was pinning it down with the sharp end of the branch in order to pull out the leg of the hen, which had been swallowed up to the thigh, while the hen flapped and cackled hysterically.

Pokuwaa was aware of a sense of triumph. If the black snake was a bad spirit, or a man turned into a snake, it had been conquered.

The first round of her battle was over. A prayer was on her lips as she ran the whole way home:

'Okatakyi Brempong,
Leader of men, linguist of all gods.
You know the deep and see what comes.
The rest of the fight is in your hand.
Okatakyi, my praises of you will never end.'

When she arrived breathless in her compound, Kwadwo Fordwuo was standing there, waiting.

'Come,' she panted, 'I'll tell you about all this when we're on our way. We are lucky to be getting there at all. I'll fetch my eggs.'

From A Woman in Her Prime, by Samuel Asare Konadu, Heinemann Educational Books Ltd., 1967.

HAUSA TALES

Translated by H. A. S. Johnston

Tatsuniyoyi Na Hausa is the title of a large collection of Hausa tales, proverbs, and other traditional material. It is probably the largest repository of African folklore in any language. The original manuscripts were collected at the turn of the century by two British administrators in Africa, Frank Edgar and John Alder Burdon. These handwritten manuscripts filled three shelves, each five feet long. By this monumental labour of love and scholarship, a cultural treasure was preserved before it could be spoiled by Western influences.

H. A. S. Johnston has drawn on this source and other smaller collections, as well as some oral sources, for his own compilation and translation, *A Selection of Hausa Stories*, from which these two Hausa tales have been taken. 'The Man with the Ugly Wife' has its counterparts in other folk literature, but 'The Severed Head' appears only in Mr Johnston's own collection. It is a good example of the Hausa's macabre sense of humour.

The Hausa people are the largest ethnic group in Northern Nigeria, and the second largest on the African continent. They are a trading and farming people whose language is used as the *lingua franca* in Nigeria and in many neighbouring countries. The Hausa language, which combines simplicity and richness, is spoken by an estimated twenty million people. It is used not only by traders but by radio stations which reach into remote villages.

The Man with the Ugly Wife

There was once a man who was married to a very plain wife, in fact the ugliest woman in the town. They were so poor that the husband had no decent gown to wear, the wife had no wraps, and they never had more than a day's food in the house.

One day the husband set about building a hut apart from the rest of the house. When he had finished he said to his wife: 'I'm going to go into this hut now and when I'm inside I want you to block up the entrance for me. I mean to live the life of a hermit for forty days and forty nights.'

When the man had shut himself up in the hut his wife sealed up the door with clay. He then spent all his days and nights in prayer and fasting. On the very last night of his vigil, however, he went to sleep and had a dream. In his dream he learnt that he could pray for three things and that whatever he prayed for would be granted to him.

Early next morning, as his time was up, he called to his wife to open the door and let him out. So she took a mattock and hacked down the clay wall which she had built over the door and released him. 'My prayers have been answered,' he said. 'For forty days and forty nights I prayed and fasted and on the last night of all I had a dream and in that dream it was revealed to me that I might pray for three things and that whatever I prayed for would be granted to me.'

When his wife had time to think about what he had told her she went to him and said: 'You know that I have no looks and am the ugliest woman in town and so I want you to pray for me to become beautiful.'

At nightfall the husband began to pray that the wife might become beautiful and, lo and behold, in the morning she had changed. She was now of surpassing softness and beauty so that in all the town there was not a woman to match her.

This news was soon carried to the palace. 'Indeed?' said the Chief when he heard of it. 'Well bring her here then. What are you waiting for?' So the woman was seized by force and carried off to the palace.

When the husband first discovered that he had lost his wife to the Chief he was in despair. Later, however, he remembered that in all three prayers had been granted to him. He therefore prayed that his wife should be changed into a monkey.

Meanwhile in the palace the Chief was just preparing to go to his new bride when his people came running in to tell him to go and see what had happened to her. The Chief followed them to the woman's room and there instead of a bride he found a monkey sitting on the bed. He was very angry and ordered his slaves to take it away. They carried it to the husband's house and dumped it there.

When the husband found that his wife had indeed been changed into a monkey he prayed that she should be restored to her former self. His prayer was answered and she turned into the same ugly woman that she had been before.

Later the husband prayed for food and clothes and other things that he and his wife needed but his prayers were not answered because he had already used the three prayers which had been promised to him in his dream. 'In this world,' he said to himself 'one thing is certain: any man who takes the advice of a woman will come to no good.'

The Severed Head

A traveller was once making his way through the bush when he came upon a severed head standing on a tree stump beside the path. He was about to pass when the head said: 'Whatever you do, learn to keep your mouth shut.'

The traveller stopped in surprise and the head repeated:

'That's what I said – learn to keep your mouth shut.'

The traveller ran away in terror and when he reached the next town he went to the palace and asked to see the Chief.

'Why do you want to see the Chief?' asked the men at the gate.

'I have something very important to tell,' said the traveller.

After a time, therefore, the traveller was admitted to the audience chamber where the Chief was sitting on his throne surrounded by his courtiers.

'God give you long life,' said the traveller, making his obeisance.

'Amen,' said the Chief. 'I hear that you have important news for me. Be sure that it is true, not false, or you will suffer for it.'

'Oh, it's true enough,' said the traveller and proceeded to tell the Chief of the severed head which he had seen on the road and of how it had opened its mouth and spoken to him.

'Have you any witnesses?' asked the Chief.

'God give you long life,' said the traveller. 'I was alone and have no witness but I left the head lying on a tree stump by the road and perhaps it will speak again.'

'Very well, 'said the Chief, 'let us test the truth of your story. If it proves to be true we will reward you but if it proves to be false you shall pay for the falsehood with your own head.'

So saying the Chief ordered the executioner and some of his henchmen to go out with the traveller and find the head. 'If the head speaks,' he said, 'bring it back here and I shall reward this man. But if it doesn't speak you are to execute him on the spot.'

So the Chief's henchmen escorted the traveller back along the same road and when they reached the tree stump they found that the severed head was still there. They gathered round it and waited for it to speak but nothing happened.

'Well anyway,' said the traveller, 'it spoke to me before.'

'That may be,' said the executioner, 'but you heard what our orders were.'

They waited again but the head made no sound.

'For God's sake say something,' cried the traveller.

Silence.

'Come on,' said the executioner, 'we're wasting our time.'

'Just give me a bit longer,' said the traveller, 'and perhaps it will speak. It did before, I swear.'

They waited again and again there was silence.

'That's enough now,' said the executioner, 'let's get it over.'

So the traveller's hands were tied behind his back and he was made to kneel on the ground. The executioner then drew his sword and with one stroke cut his head off.

As the traveller's head rolled to the ground, the head on the tree stump at last spoke out.

'There you are,' it said. 'I told him before to keep his mouth shut.'

Chief Sekoto Holds Court

by Bessie Head

Bessie Head, born in South Africa in 1937, knows nothing about her parents. She was educated in a missionary orphanage in Durban and trained as an elementary school teacher. After several years as a teacher, she worked on the staff of *Drum*, an English-language magazine which became the proving ground for many African writers. When her life in South Africa became too frustrating, she emigrated to Botswana, the former Bechuanaland.

Of her adopted country she writes, 'I really liked this country from the very day I came here. I have always been lonely and to me it was just like a fish finding a pond at last. A country like this forces you to find your underground spring in order to survive.'

'Chief Sekoto Holds Court' is taken from Bessie Head's first novel, *When the Rain Clouds Gather*, an inspiring story of Botswana in transition from the old tribal ways and colonial domination to a new way of life.

Even those who did not like chiefs had to concede that Paramount Chief Sekoto was a very charming man. His charm lay not so much in his outer appearance as in his very cheerful outlook on life. In fact, so fond was he of the sunny side of life that he was inclined to regard any gloomy, pessimistic person as insane and make every effort to avoid his company. It was his belief that a witty answer turneth away wrath and that the oil of reason should always be poured on troubled waters.

Every weekday morning, Chief Sekoto listened to cases brought before his court, while the afternoons were spent at leisure unless there were people who had made appointments to interview him. This particular Monday morning a lively and rowdy case was in session when, out of the corner of his eye, Chief Sekoto saw his brother Matenge drive up and park his car opposite the open clearing where court was held. Nothing upset Chief Sekoto more than a visit from his brother, whom he had long classified as belonging to the insane part of mankind. He determined to dally over the proceedings for as long as possible in the hope that his brother would become bored and leave. Therefore he turned his full attention on the case at hand.

The case had been brought in from one of the outlying villages, called Bodibeng, and the cause of its rowdiness was that the whole village of Bodibeng had turned up to witness the trial. A certain old woman of the village, named Mma-Baloi, was charged with allegedly practising witchcraft, and so certain were the villagers of her guilt that they frequently forgot themselves and burst out into loud chatter and had to be brought to order by the president of the court with threats of fines.

Evidence was that Mma-Baloi had always lived a secret and mysterious life apart from the other villagers. She was also in the habit of receiving strangers from far-off places into her home who would not state what dealings they had with Mma-Baloi. Now, over a certain period, a number of the children of the village had died sudden deaths, and each time a mother stood up to describe these sudden deaths the crowd roared in fury because the deaths of the children and the evil practices of Mma-Baloi were one and the same thing in their minds. The accused, Mma-Baloi, sat a little apart from the villagers in a quaking, ashen, crumpled heap; and each time the villagers roared, she seemed about to sink into the earth. Noting this, Chief Sekoto's kindly heart was struck with pity.

Further evidence was that about a week ago a strange young woman had turned up in the village of Bodibeng and made straight for the hut of Mma-Baloi, where she had died a sudden death. This had made Mma-Baloi run screaming from her hut, and it was only the intervention of the police that had saved Mma-Baloi from being torn to pieces by the villagers.

Chief Sekoto was silent for some time. The insanity of mankind never ceased to amaze him. At last he turned to the accused and said gently, 'Well, mother, what do you have to say in defence of yourself?'

'Sir, I am no witch,' said the quavering old voice. 'Even though I am called the mother of the witches, I am no witch. Long ago I was taught by the people who live in the bush how to cure ailments with herbs and that is my business.'

She pointed a shaking finger at a bag placed near her.

'I would like to see the contents of the bag,' Chief Sekoto said with a great show of interest. The bag was brought to him and its contents tipped out on the ground. They were a various assortment of dried leaves, roots, and berries. He examined them leisurely, picking up a few items for closer inspection. This very deliberate gesture was meant to puncture a hole in the confidence of the crowd, who annoyed him. While he fiddled about he was aware of how silent and intent they had become, following his every movement with their eyes. Thus holding the stage, he turned to the old woman and said:

'Proceed with your defence, mother.'

'About the deaths of the children of which I am accused, I know nothing, sir,' she said. 'About the young woman who died in my home last Saturday, I am also innocent. This young woman came to me on recommendation, being grievously ill. We were discussing the ailment when she fell dead at my feet. Never has such a thing occurred before, and this caused me to lose my mind and run out of the house.'

'That is quite understandable, mother,' Chief Sekoto said sympathetically. 'Even I should have been grieved if some stranger was struck with death in my home.'

He swept the crowd with a stern glance. 'Who issues the certificates of death in Bodibeng?' he asked.

There was a short, bewildered silence. Then a car and a messenger had to be found to fetch the doctor of the Bodibeng hospital. There was a delay of two hours as the doctor was engaged in an operation. Throughout this long wait the court remained in session. At one stage Chief Sekoto received an impatient note: 'Dear Brother,' it said. 'Please spare a few moments to discuss an urgent matter.'

Chief Sekoto replied: 'Is it life or death? I am at the moment faced with the life or death of an old woman. I cannot move.'

It was near noon when the doctor arrived. His evidence was brief and to the point. Yes, it was true, he said. There had been a surprising number of child deaths in the village of Bodibeng, and death in each case had been due to pneumonia; and yes, he said, he had performed a postmortem last Saturday afternoon. The young woman had died of a septic womb due to having procured an abortion with a hooked and unsterilized instrument. He would say that the septic condition of the womb had been of three months' duration.

All that was left now was for Chief Sekoto to pass judgment on the case. This he did sternly, drawing himself up to his full height.

'People of Bodibeng,' he said. 'It seems to me you are all suffering from derangement of the brain.'

He paused long enough to allow the villagers to look at each other uneasily.

'Your children die of pneumonia,' he thundered, 'and to shield yourselves from blame you accuse a poor old woman of having bewitched them into death. Not only that. You falsely accuse her of a most serious crime which carries the death sentence. How long have you planned the death of a poor old woman, deranged people of Bodibeng? How long have you caused her to live in utter misery, suspicion, and fear? I say: Can dogs bark for ever? Oh no, people of Bodibeng, today you will make payment for the legs of the old mother who has fled before your barking. I say: The fault is all with you, and because of this I fine each household of Bodibeng one beast. From the money that arises out of the sale of these beasts, each household is to purchase warm clothing for the children so that they may no longer die of pneumonia.'

He turned and looked at the old woman, changing his expression to one of kindness.

'As for you, mother,' he said. 'I cannot allow you to go and live once more among the people of Bodibeng. It is only hatred that the people of Bodibeng feel for you, and this has driven them out of their minds. As hatred never dies, who knows what evil they will not plot against you. I have a large house, and you are welcome to the protection it offers. Besides, I suffer from an ailment for which I am always given penicillin injections at the hospital. Now I am tired of the penicillin injections and perhaps your good herbs may serve to cure me of my troubles.'

He stood up, signifying the end of the case. The people of Bodibeng fled in confusion from the courtyard, but the old woman sat for a long time on the ground, silent tears of gratitude dripping down into her lap.

From When Rain Clouds Gather, *by Bessie Head, Simon & Schuster, Inc., 1968.*

How a Devil Danced to Death

by A. Doris Banks Henries

A. Doris Banks Henries was assisted by students at the University of Liberia and by tribal storytellers from the back country in writing down the ninety-nine stories which make up her collection of Liberian folklore.

Tribal literature in Liberia, as in other African countries, was passed by word of mouth until the twentieth century, and even now very little has been written down. For one thing, there are the different tribal languages: the Vai in the northwest, the Kru along the coast, the Golas in the west-central, and the Kpelle in the centre and northwest. In addition, there are tales told by the Muslim traders and the Fanti fishermen from Ghana who travel back and forth.

So it is not surprising that the tales of many West African countries are similar. There are varying themes among the tales. Some are morality tales of trickery and foolishness. Many are animal stories, in which the animal characters vary, depending on the region. Where insects are present in great numbers, the spider or the fly or the cockroach assumes human characteristics. And in most of the tales inhabitants of the spirit world – witches, ghosts, devils, and demons – play important roles.

A devil wandered through the forest until he came to a place where two big roads crossed. There he built himself a little house. This was a bad thing for the people who used these roads, for devils are wicked and devour human beings.

When anyone came to the cross-roads, the devil would jump out of his house on the corner, holding a drum under his arm. He would beat the drum and command the wayfarer to dance.

'Dance, O Man! Dance and I will play the drum for you.

He who tires first must die!'

The unfortunate traveller, whether he was a man, woman or child, would be obliged to dance a Dance of Death, for invariably the dancer tired first and was killed and eaten by the devil.

Men know that twins often have unusual powers. They make fine magicians and medicine men. They are wise in telling fortunes and know the use of herbs and poison. A pair of twins decided they would outwit and kill the devil who had killed many people from their town. They left their town one morning to see what they could do. One of them crept ahead very softly and hid behind an anthill close to the devil's house. Then his brother boldly approached singing a pleasant song.

The devil heard him coming and jumped from his house. 'Ho!' he cried in great delight. He had not seen a man for days. 'Ho, young man! Come and dance for me!' The devil began beating excitedly on his drum.

'Thank you, sir,' said the lad. 'It is a fine morning for a dance. Play on!'

The devil threw back his head and laughed at such insolence. 'Do you know, youth, that the one of us who tires first must die?'

'Fine,' said the twin. 'That means the other one will live.' He danced and danced to the devil's drumming or playing. When he was tired, he skipped behind the anthill and his brother skipped out in his place. In this fashion the twins danced for three whole days; whenever one was dancing, the other one was resting. The devil was astonished to see, as he thought, one person dance on and on, day and night and he himself grew tired. The twins continued to change places. The devil dropped, wilted and at last he fell exhausted on the ground.

The twins killed the devil by cutting his body into two parts. They impaled one half on a stake and carried it into town. There it stayed as a warning to all devils that twins lived in that place and would tolerate no wicked devil tricks.

The Television-handed Ghostess

by Amos Tutuola

Amos Tutuola was born in 1920, a member of the Yoruba
tribe in Nigeria. He was educated at a Christian missionary
school and then became a coppersmith. He began to write in
English, in an unspoiled, vigorous style, full of fantasy and
imagination. He chose as his theme the African belief in
ghosts and witchcraft, and has woven into his books much
traditional mythology and supernatural imagery.

His first book, *The Palm-Wine Drinkard* (1952), established
him as a master of storytelling in the oral tradition. Dylan
Thomas called it 'grisly and bewitching.' There is both horror
and comedy in his story of the drinker of palm wine
who set out to explore the world of the dead. The same is
true of his two later books, *My Life in the Bush of Ghosts*
and *Simbi and the Satyr of the Dark Jungle*. Tutuola's
use of English is often primitive and jarring, but his message
comes through, loud and clear.

The following episode is taken from his second and
probably most famous book, *My Life in the Bush of Ghosts*. The
young hero, a boy of seven, flees from home to escape
a slave raid and plunges into worse dangers in the ghost-
ridden African bush. Tutuola's ghosts, like Fagunwa's,
are not the ethereal ghosts of the western world, but evil
demons – hideous, dirty, and smelly, and totally fearsome.
The boy in the story is dragged fearfully through one
ghost town after another for twenty-four years, until he meets
the television-handed ghostess.

When it was about two o'clock P.M. I saw a ghostess who
was crying bitterly and coming to me direct in a hut where
I laid down enjoying myself. When she entered I noticed
that she held a short mat which was woven with dried weeds.

She was not more than three feet high, Immediately she entered she went direct to the fire, she spread the mat closely to the fire and then sat down on it without saluting or talking to me. So at this stage I noticed carefully that she was almost covered with sores, even there was no single hair on her head, except sores with uncountable maggots which were dashing here and there on her body. Both her arms were not more than one and a half foot, it had uncountable short fingers. She was crying bitterly and repeatedly as if somebody was stabbing her with knives.

Of course, I did not talk to her, but I was looking at her with much astonishment until I saw the water of her eyes that it was near to quench the fire, then I got up with anger and told her to walk out of my hut, because if the water quenches the fire I should not be able to get another again, as there were not matches in the Bush of Ghosts. But instead of walking out as I said she started to cry louder than ever. When I could not bear her cry I asked her – 'by the way what are you crying for?' She replied – 'I am crying because of you.' Then I asked – 'because of me?' She said – 'yes' and I said – 'What for?' Then she started to relate her story thus –

'I was born over two hundred years ago with sores on my head and all over my body. Since the day that I was born I have no other work more than to find out the doctor who could heal it for me and several of them had tried all their best but failed. Instead of healing or curing it would be spreading wider and then giving me more pains. I have been to many sorcerers to know whether the sore would be healed, but every one of them was telling me that there is an earthly person who had been lost in this Bush of Ghosts, so that if I can be wandering about I might see you one day, and the sorcerers said that if you will be licking the sore every day with your tongue for ten years it would be healed.

'So that I am very lucky and very glad that I meet you here today and I shall also be exceedingly glad if you will be licking the sore with your tongue every day until the ten years that it will be healed as the sorcerers had told me. And I am also crying bitterly in respect of you because I believe that no doubt you have been struggling for many years in this Bush of Ghosts for the right way to your home town, but you are seeing the way every day and you do not know it, because every earthly person gets eyes but cannot see. Even it is on the right way to your home town that you found this hut and sleep or sit in it every day and night. Although I believe that you will not refuse to lick the sore until it is healed.'

Having related her story and said that if I am licking the sore it would be healed as the sorcerer said, so I replied – ' I want you to go back to your sorcerers and tell them I refuse to lick the sore.' After I told her like this she said again – 'It is not a matter of going back to the sorcerers, but if you can do it look at my palm or hand.' But when she told me to look at her palm and opened it nearly to touch my face, it was exactly as a television, I saw my town, mother, brother and all my playmates, then she was asking me frequently – 'do you agree to be licking the sore with your tongue, tell me, now, yes or no?'

Because when I thought over how the sore was dirty and smelling badly, especially those maggots which were dashing here and there all over the sore, so it was hard for me to say 'yes.' But as I was seeing my town with all my people, it was hard for me to say 'No.' But as I was hearing on this television when my mother was discussing about me with one of her friends with a sorrowful voice at that time that – 'She was told by a fortune teller that I am still alive in a bush.' So as I was enjoying these discussions the television-handed ghostess took away the hand from my face and I saw nothing again except the hand.

After that she asked again whether I would do her request, of course. I was unable to answer at that moment, but only thinking about my people whom I saw on the television and also thinking how to reach the town as quickly as possible. But as it was just a dream for me, I told her again to let me look at them once more before I would answer her request. Immediately she showed it to me my people appeared again at the same time and as I was looking at them and also hearing what they were talking about me which I ought to answer if I was with them, luckily, a woman brought her baby who had a sore on its foot to my mother at that time to tell her the kind of leaf which could heal the sore. But as my mother knows many kinds of leaves which can heal any sore, so she told this woman to follow her. Having reached a small bush which is near the town, then she cut many leaves on a kind of plant and gave them to this woman, after that she told her that she must warm the leaves in hot water before using it for the sore. But as I was looking at them on the television I knew the kind of leaf and also heard the direction how to use it.

After a while this 'Television-handed ghostess' took her hand away from my face and I saw nothing again. Then she asked again whether I would do her request, so I said — 'Yes, but not with my tongue would I heal the sore.' After I said 'yes' I got out of the hut and I went round near the hut. God is so good, this kind of leaf or plant were full up there. Then I cut some and came back to the hut, after that I was using it for the sore according to the direction that my mother told the woman who brought her baby to her. It was so I was using these leaves for the sore every day and to my surprise, this sore had been healed within a week. But when this 'Television-handed ghostess' saw that she had no more sores again she was exceedingly glad.

Having eaten and drunk to my satisfaction I told her to tell me the right way to my home town as she had promised me before I healed her sore. She agreed, but warned me seriously that I must not attempt to enter into the Bush of Ghosts forever, because ninety percent of ghosts hate any of the earthly persons to enter this bush, as I myself am aware of it since I have been struggling to find the right way back to my town, but none of the merciless ghosts would show me the way. After the above warning she said further — 'Do not tell anybody that I am the "Television-handed ghostess" who shows you the right way whenever you reach your town.' Then she opened her palm as usual, she told me to look at it, but to my surprise, I simply found myself under the fruit tree which is near my home town (the Future-Sign). It was under this fruit tree my brother left me on the road when he was running away from the enemies' guns which were driving me farther and farther until I entered into the Bush of Ghosts, and it was the fruit of this tree I ate first immediately I entered the Bush of Ghosts. This is how I got out of the Bush of Ghosts, which I entered when I was seven years old.

From My Life in the Bush of Ghosts, *by Amos Tutuola, Faber and Faber Ltd., London, 1954, and Grove Press Inc., 1970.*

I See a Lonely Dead

by Prince Modupe

Prince Modupe was born on the Guinea Coast, a member of the Susu (or So-So) tribe. At an early age, young Modupe left his native village in search of education and studied at a missionary school in Freetown. By the time he grew up, he had become interested in seeing the world outside of Africa. In 1922 he travelled to the United States and studied at Hampton Institute in Virginia. Later he married an American and settled in California. He became a filmwriter, actor, and lecturer on African subjects.

When his American-born children were small, he told them stories of his childhood. He showed them scars on his body which were the marks of initiation into the Leopard Society. When they begged for these stories over and over, he wrote some of them down in a book called *I Was a Savage*, recently reissued under the title *A Royal Prince*. More than fifty years have passed, some names have been changed, and perhaps not all of the incidents are strictly autobiographical. But this story of 'a lonely dead' could very well be true.

When my father returned from his long overland trading trips, his clothing was always stained with the dust of the journey. There was in the cloth the smells of the cargo he carried – hides, ground nuts (peanuts), cola. I knew these

things came from places which were only names to me—
Bomako, Kauroussa, Kankan. They seemed as remote as
the moon, and this made the odours seem exotic. The smell
of leather was the smell of travel. I inhaled it as I walked
one morning beside him, his country-cloth robe fluttering in
the breeze, flapping against my face. He was taking me to
call on my grandfather.

We were in the prayer room when a messenger arrived
from the Bambara tribe. I retreated with my father to a far
corner of the room while my grandfather granted audience.
Before my eyes, I saw the familiar, kindly old grandfather
become the stern, majestic chief attending to important
affairs.

Africans are a ceremonious people. There were long polite
inquiries. The health of everybody? I could see that the
messenger was fairly bristling with excitement under the
calm surface of politeness. I hoped Grandfather would forget
my presence in the room. I wanted to know what this was
about!

They finally got around to the point and exciting enough
it was! A *lappa* had been stolen from the house of a Bambara
woman. A So-So warrior had been seen running from
the village with something in his hand which resembled a
lappa.

Theft was almost unknown among our people. It was
punishable by death. If the Bambara were mistaken, if the
accusation were false, tribal war would follow. If they
were correct, if one of our people had stolen, the guilty
So-So would have to be discovered and punished.

Grandfather's voice was terrible to hear. It was sort of a
growl with a crack in it. Was the name of the So-So youth
known to the Bambaras?

The witch doctor had called the name, a youth known as
Santigi.

I felt my father stiffen. I no longer wanted to be in that
room but I dared not move. Santigi!

Santigi was betrothed to my sister N'gadi. The marriage
had been arranged except for one detail—Santigi had not
accumulated all of the necessary dowry. The part he lacked

was a bright new *lappa*, the wrap-around skirt which tribal women wear.

Tribesmen do not 'buy' their brides. The dowry is a sort of marriage insurance. It means that the man appreciates the value of the girl and he wants to make a token of this appreciation to the girl's parents. It is the tangible way to show his respect for the girl and her family.

Santigi was not rich, even by bush standards, but he was strong and hard-working, and fearless, a well-liked fellow. My sister N'gadi loved him and he was acceptable to our family. N'gadi was studying to be a medicine woman and already had her own house away from ours.

Grandfather dispatched a messenger to fetch Santigi to the prayer room where we waited. The silence in the room seemed jungle heavy. Neither my grandfather nor the Bambara spoke.

When Santigi came in, after what seemed a long time, he stood straight and proud. He seemed to fill the doorway as he came through it. The questioning began. Had Santigi been to the Bambara town?

Santigi nodded, easily enough. He had gone to the Bambara market.

Why had he gone to a Bambara market? Was not every needful thing to be had in our own market?

He had gone to look for a fine bright new *lappa*! He got over the word *lappa* without a pause.

He brought a *lappa* back with him? He shook his whole body with his head. No *lappa*!

There was nothing for it now but trial by ordeal. That was the tribal way of establishing innocence. One's innocence was one's protection. If after drinking the judgment poison, a brew called *wobia*, Santigi was able to keep his feet under him, war would follow. The Bambara's witch doctor's word would have been challenged. The Bambara were a powerful tribe.

There was a great commotion among our people when the word got around. Some of the more excitable thought the warriors might as well get their weapons ready. It seemed unlikely that Santigi would steal, even more unlikely that he would be able to steal and then lie about it without a quiver of guilt showing in his face.

Excitement kept sleep away from me that night. I thought about N'Gadi, the way she would feel if Santigi did not survive the judgment poison. N'Gadi was thin as early-morning shadow and not robust in any part except her spirit which was staunch. She was probably sobbing alone in her medicine hut, forgotten in the turmoil by everyone except myself.

I thought about war, how exciting that would be, how disgusting that I was less than warrior age. How unspeakable to be left at home with women and children, probably hiding out in the forest in case our town should be taken.

I thought about Santigi. Would he be alive or dead after another sundown? If the poison caught him, and he were buried face down as criminals are, N'gadi would have to watch this disgrace. I wondered how it would feel to be dead, a dead criminal, unable to join the spirits of the reverenced dead, how lonely. How would a lonely dead feel when the feast was made to the spirits of deceased elders and he could not join the festival. I knew that a man who lives the laws of his tribe is never alone, living or dead. Surely Santigi had not risked becoming a lonely dead, not even for love of N'gadi!

Death was interesting to think about. I tried to imagine that the dark hut was a grave, that the *canda* mat beneath me was a burial mat. People would sing praise-songs over me, recounting deeds of great valour . . . N'gadi in mournful sing-song telling how I had saved her from a terror of a Bambara warrior . . .

N'gadi! Everything I thought about led my mind to my sister. I had given myself the shivers thinking about death. I wanted to feel the comfort of my sister's arms around me. I would run to N'gadi. Night is the roaming time of spirits and it would be terrifying to go out alone at night. I was so frightened by the thoughts I had been thinking that I had to leave them behind in this hut, so I would make a dash for it. In no time at all I would be with N'gadi and we could sob together.

No one stirred as I slipped out the door. Moonlight flooded

the village but I stayed clear of it by moving between huts until my sister's house and the medicine man's behind it were the only ones to be seen in front of me.

I was gathering up my courage for the final spurt of distance when I saw a figure moving stealthily as a leopard toward the medicine man's hut. The figure was a woman and she carried a gourd carefully so as not to spill the contents. The figure was slim like N'gadi. In fact, it almost certainly was N'gadi! Was it her spirit walking? The figure disappeared behind the medicine hut for only as long as it takes an elephant to trumpet. When she reappeared there was still a gourd in her hands.

I slipped back to my *canda* as quickly as I could get there. I had seen something which no one should have looked upon because it should not have happened. I did not understand it but I knew it was evil. Curled up into a small ball of frightened humanity, I finally fell asleep.

The drums began talking early the next morning. As soon as the Bambara arrived, the people gathered for the trial. Santigi was at the centre of a great circle, surrounded by elders and warriors and the witch doctor. My sister was there but I was afraid to meet her eyes. She had strange powers which I feared.

The witch doctor poured the *wobia* from a gourd into a larger pot over the fire. He talked to the steaming juice. The drums beat loud and fast, then ceased. All sound and motion ceased with the drums. In the silence, the witch doctor reached out a calabash full of the hot liquid to Santigi. I could not tell whether Santigi's hand shook or whether it only seemed to because of the heat waves above the poison pot. He planted his legs far apart as though to brace himself upright. He watched N'gadi as he drained the calabash. N'gadi looked at the ground. Everyone else seemed intent on Santigi. He seemed to sway once but quickly recovered himself. It was finally apparent to everyone that the poison was not going to topple him.

My grandfather stood up. The Bambara stood up. My grandfather spoke in a harsh voice. The warrior had proven his innocence. If war had to come, we were ready.

Santigi's friends swarmed around him, whooping their

joy – all but N'gadi. She walked home with the rest of my family and was strangely quiet.

It was after the midday resting time when some exciting news went around the town. Matara, my mother, had dozed and dreamed that *uba*, the vulture, had perched in her house. There is no omen more terrible than this. Calamity of the worst sort is sure to follow. What had it to do with the strange thing I had seen in the moonlight? I must speak.

I found my father alone. His face became grim when I told him what I had to say. His first thought was to ask N'gadi whether she had substituted some innocent brew for the powerful *wobia*. Talking to himself rather than to me, he changed his mind. He would ask Santigi. He would tell Santigi of the ruin that was sure to fall on all of the people, even on N'gadi, if he had done an evil he would not confess.

We heard the message drums that evening: Santigi guilty ... Santigi to die ... Santigi guilty ... Santigi to die ... We have lappa ... Santigi to die.

People gathered quickly in the central compound, Santigi in the centre of the throng, his head bowed. The witch doctor held up a bright new *lappa* so that all could see it before Grandfather dispatched a runner to carry it to the Bambara town.

The witch doctor explained that the power of the *wobia* had been crossed. Santigi had confessed to this as well as to the stealing and lying – all terrible crimes. N'gadi's lips were parted. I was afraid she was going to declare herself. I saw that Santigi was looking at N'gadi too. Ever so slightly, he shook his head at her. There was great pride in both of them as they stared at one another across the space which separated them.

Santigi was to die three sundowns hence. From the time Grandfather announced the execution until it was carried out, the *taboole*, the sacred drums of sorrow, never ceased throbbing. They spoke slowly at first, gathering pace gradually as the death hour approached. Their voice seemed like great sobs, yet they were more sorrowful than anything that could come from a human throat. The vibrations shuddered the earth beneath our feet and I thought that the earth itself joined in the crushing lament.

By the third day no one found it possible to do any work. The call to sorrow and shame was too urgent. The adults went about with set, sad faces. For the first time in my childhood the days seemed long, endless. The death chant was taken up all through the town. A great many friends and relatives of Santigi's overflowed his home. As many as could find seating room on the floor wailed there and threw ashes over their heads. I looked for N'gadi but she was nowhere about. My mother stayed in her house grieving over the sin of the youth who was to die because he loved her daughter above the laws of the tribe.

As the execution time neared, all women and children were shooed toward their homes. The women would continue their lament behind closed doors. What was to be done was not a thing for children to see.

I hid behind the trunk of a tree. In my overexcited imagination I had already witnessed the execution a hundred times over. I felt strangely a part of what was going on. If I had not told my father what I had seen in the moonlight, the warriors might at that moment have been going to war instead of to the sacrifice rock. I was horribly fascinated by this affair I had stumbled into and I wanted to stay with it to the end.

It was easy during the confusion to manœuvre my way from tree to tree until I neared the great rock. The sacrifice altar was screened by trees. I scrambled up one of them and fastened myself tight against a horizontal limb.

The fire in the centre of the clearing was burning brightly when I attained my lookout perch, but the death procession had not reached the place.

Boom . . . Boom, boom, boom . . . My tree trembled with the thuds. War drums joined in with the drums of sorrow.

Warriors of his own age group escorted Santigi to a spot in front of the sacred rock. They were dressed in full regalia, hide shields, spears, plumed headgear. The dancing firelight glinted on the edges of the spears. The warriors formed a circle, leaving an opening for the entry of the older men, the tribal elders, the witch doctor, the executioner. These two came in last, wearing masks. The executioner carried a long, broad knife, curved on the end. It is called a sacrifice knife because this really was a sacrifice that was about to be made – the sacrifice of a life to the sacred principles of tribal law. The masks embodied the spirit of that law as it had come down to us from the ancient ones who had died, yet who live forever through the laws and the customs.

Santigi's expression was resigned as the warriors bound him. He must have thought that the best he could do was to die like a true tribesman, he who had not been able to live as one. Perhaps by this last bit of brave living he would be allowed to sit on the far edge of the conclave of tribal dead.

The warriors danced, spears in hand. At the edge of the circle was a large calabash filled with palm wine to which herbs of strange powers had been added. This was taken in great gulps by the dancers as the tempo of the drumming and dancing increased. The longer they danced, the higher they leaped, the faster they whirled. The light and heavy drums, combined with the thud of feet and the chorus of chant, shook the tree where I perched. I dug my hands into the bark of the branch. If I fell like a ripe fruit, the executioner might have double duty that night!

Sweat gleamed on the bodies of the frenzied dancers, their eyes rolled, some of them were overcome with paroxysmal spasms and fell at the edge of the circle with foam on their lips.

The executioner did not dance. He stood with folded arms looking down at Santigi. When the big drum stopped, every sound and movement stopped with it. The executioner grasped the end of the knife with both hands, raised it high and swung. After that single sweeping motion, Santigi's head rolled sideways. A gush of blood rose out of his neck. The sacred rock was red.

The drums came to life again. The booming was no longer frenzied, but sad, so sad. I wanted to sob. Santigi who had always seemed to me to be so much of one piece, his whole body springing forward to run, to leap, to wrestle, to dance, Santigi was severed. Boy that I was, I understood that even as his head was separated from his body, his soul was separated from the body of his tribe. That, not his death, was the real horror of what I had seen.

From I was a Savage, by Prince Modupe, Harcourt Brace Jovanovich, Inc., 1957.

IMAGES OF DEATH

In tribal Africa, death is neither the end of life nor the gateway to immortality. It is rather a stepping stone between generations, a link with one's ancestors and one's descendants.

Ulli Beier, founder and editor of the magazine *Black Orpheus*, in commenting on the theme of the ancestors in African poetry, writes: 'The living and the dead are in continuous contact and a large part of the religious life of the African is devoted to establishing a harmonious contact with the dead.'

In the three poems which follow, anonymous poets from the Yoruba, the Baulé, and the Kuba tribes record their feelings and attitudes toward death.

The God of War

He kills on the right and destroys on the left.
He kills on the left and destroys on the right.
He kills suddenly in the house and suddenly in the field.
He kills the child with the iron with which it plays.
He kills in silence.
He kills the thief and the owner of the stolen goods.
He kills the owner of the slave – and the slave runs away.
He kills the owner of the house – and paints the hearth with
  his blood.
He is the needle that pricks at both ends.
He has water but he washes with blood.

Yoruba Tribe

The Sorrow of Kodio

We were three women
Three men
And myself, Kodio Ango.
We were on our way to work in the city.
And I lost my wife Nanama on the way.
I alone have lost my wife
To me alone such misery has happened,
To me alone, Kodio, the most handsome of the three men,
Such misery has happened.
In vain I call for my wife,
She died on the way like a chicken running.
How shall I tell her mother?
How shall I tell it to her, I Kodio,
When it is so hard to hold back my own pain.

Baulé Tribe

Death

There is no needle without piercing point.
There is no razor without trenchant blade.
Death comes to us in many forms.

With our feet we walk the goat's earth.
With our hands we touch God's sky.
Some future day in the heat of noon,
I shall be carried shoulder high
through the village of the dead.
When I die, don't bury me under forest trees,
I fear their thorns.
When I die, don't bury me under forest trees.
I fear the dripping water.
Bury me under the great shade trees in the market,
I want to hear the drums beating
I want to feel the dancers' feet.

Kuba Tribe

Part 2

Village Voices

If relatives help each other,
what evil can hurt them?
Ethiopian Proverb

Kenya Our Motherland

by John Mbiti

Beneath these mortal feet
Is motherland,
Our Kenya Motherland
Freed in tears and blood,
The hump of Africa
Soaring skyways amid the clouds,
Forever wearing the white cap
Like a covenant knot upon th' equator,
A sentry among the clouds
Forever pointing us to God,
For us soliciting rain
The blessed milk of African life.

Beneath thy heavenw'd heights
Tumble down the depths
That mark the Great Crack,
The scar of God's great axe
That split the rocks by force
Igniting fire beneath volcanic hills.

Oh Kenya Motherland,
Where flamingoes roost on sanctuary lakes,
And lions sunk in deep, deep slumber
Awake to the tune of hooting cars;
From whose eastern shores
Ever pounding waves scrub thy rocky ribs;
In whose northern desert land
Sand dunes roll over eternal silence
Tomorrow's cure for strained nerves.
Let God bless thee, our Motherland.

SONS OF AFRICA

John S. Kado and R. Lucy Kuria are two of the twenty secondary school students whose writings were selected for publication in a competition held in Kenya in 1966. Each student was asked to write about an experience that began with the words, 'When I awoke . . .' The Honourable James S. Gichuru, in his foreword to the book, says, 'These young writers exhibit an astonishing facility and command of the English language which my older generation cannot but envy.'

Coming of Age

by John S. Kado

When I awoke, there was an unusual silence in the air and I found myself listening for something – the sound of a warning horn. As it sounded I slipped on a skin cloak and rushed from my hut. This was an important day. A day when a group of brave youths was going to be tested and enlisted in my tribe's defence force as men. On such occasions quietness was, without reason, maintained and the early morning cry of birds rare.

'If I succeed, I will be able to act and think in love, fame and glory as men of my tribe do,' I told myself as I hurried to offer sacrifice to my dead ancestors.

'Quee! Quee! Quee!' cried the hen as I cruelly butchered it with a blunt ancestral knife. But I cared not for the cry. I was only after success. The cruel deed done, I gave the sun my back and threw the dying hen towards it – to the sun-rays. For that is where my dead ancestors lived.

Shortly I was on my way to the 'Oak of the ancestors'

where the test was to be.

'Be grateful to those who brought you up by hand, my son. Remember, it will be a mere beating of your back till blood appears,' were my father's only words of encouragement.

When I arrived, there was a big crowd waiting anxiously to see this cruel test.

Suddenly the sweet pomp of the African drums was on the beat. This evoked in me the pride of being a true son of Africa. We were summoned to stand on a line in front of the elders of our tribe. The test was about to begin. Our backs were to be beaten with whips till blood appeared. The drum-beats were to regulate the speed of beating. To show one's manliness one was not allowed to shake or cry. It was cruel.

The first boy passed well. But the second, alas, the womb that carried him! After a beating he burst out with a loud cry releasing and urinating as if his guts had no way to control the swallowed food. His father was greatly ashamed. Then came my turn. The first beating made my blood run madly around my body. I felt the pain on top of my forehead. The whole of my back was paralysed instantly. As the beating went on I felt no further pain. Then I knew that the ghosts of my dead ancestors had clustered on my back to receive the beatings. The sacrifice was good – a fat, clean hen.

'Blood!' the crowd shouted. I had passed the test. As my father and relatives rushed to hail me, I felt some deadly pain. I nearly cried but the test was over. I was a man!

I was carried home amid cheers as the test was continued on the others. My wounded back was nursed first. Then I was given the best of food – fried mutton. Meanwhile gifts poured in from my relatives, which put together made me a man of meagre wealth – enough to start life with.

After eating I went to sleep to avoid pain. I was proud to be a son of Africa. Africa the land of black proud warriors like myself in the ancestral savannah. I took opium to make me fall asleep quickly.

Out of Disaster

by R. Lucy Kuria

When I awoke, there was an unusual silence in the air and I found myself listening for something I used to hear whenever I awoke in the hot afternoons.

I then remembered how, two days before, I had been looking after my master's cattle and how two Masai warriors had come and had taken the cattle. They had beaten me savagely. They did not, however, leave me lying on the ground, half dead. Instead they managed to get me into their land somehow. I was a strong boy of twenty and I should guess that was the reason why they took me along with them. After they had beaten me, I was unconscious and did not come back to myself until the second day.

My friends and I had often fallen asleep in the hottest times of the day and when I awoke, I always heard the same sounds in the air. I always heard the sound made by flying grasshoppers ka-rrrrrrr-ah, the sound of men chopping wood with their axes in the forest near by, kong-kong-kong. The sun was always so hot that one would say it shone loudly! Its heat seemed to have a sound to me. These sounds were familiar. They were the sounds I was expecting to hear when I awoke that morning.

The two men had put me in a mud hut with no windows. The door was very small and low and the inside of the hut was very dark. I recalled what had happened and then sat in the darkness staring at nothing. Presently the door opened and three men came in followed by a beautiful girl, who had hardly anything on her body. She was carrying a gourd which she offered to me. I took it and drank it, not caring what was inside. After that the men took me outside and treated my wounds. They were kind and I liked them.

I could recognize the hills on which we were. They were the hills one saw far in the distance when at home. I hoped that when I got better, I would run away. Knowing how hard my master was at home, I could not go back to him. I would seek happiness among some other tribes.

The Masai family looked after me very well. Meat was our food. The girl I had first seen brought me milk and meat daily. We grew to like each other very much. She taught me the Masai language and I learned very quickly. After some weeks I got better, but I did not want to run away. I stayed with the family and proved to be a trustworthy man. I became one of the members of the family and took part in every event.

I remember once the two men, Muriu and Karau, who had taken the cattle, and me, went out to steal more cows. We were caught in the act by the owners. We all fought against them but I fought so bravely that afterwards when we got home, I was rewarded by the two men. They gave Ngini to me as my wife. She was the girl I had liked very much and who had made me love Masailand so much; we loved one another. I did not ever again think of leaving Masailand. I grew old and my sons carried on the work of stealing cattle. Every morning when I awoke I remembered the morning when I awoke and found myself listening for something; but the familiar sounds were lost for ever.

Exile

by Alhaji Sir Abubakar
Tafawa Balewa

Sir Abubakar Tafawa Balewa was the first Prime Minister of independent Nigeria in 1960. Educated in Nigeria and at London University, he belonged to the Hausa, an important ethnic group already introduced in this anthology (page 32). Today Hausas are devout Moslems, and Balewa was no exception. He had made the pilgrimage to Mecca and was entitled to use the title Alhaji. As a political leader, he was respected for his honesty, his tolerance, and his vision of a united Nigeria. He was accidentally killed during the military coup of January 1966.

Few people outside Nigeria know that he was a novelist as well as a political leader. He had tremendous pride in Hausa tradition and in the Islamic way of life, which he portrays in his novel *Shaihu Umar*. The story is set at the end of the nineteenth century when Arab slave caravans still ran regularly from Kano across the Sahara to Egypt. It was the custom for the Muslims to raid the neighbouring pagan tribes for slaves and cattle. They were a very pious people who believed that their activities were blessed by Allah, the god of the Muslims.

The hero is a young Hausa boy who was kidnapped and sold into slavery. Unlike the majority, he was given an education and became an Islamic *malam*, or teacher. One day, just before evening prayer, a student asked him to tell about the country from which he came, and why he had left home. It was a long story which caused pity and wonder in all who heard it. The first episode follows.

Away back (began Shaihu Umar) I was a native of this country, but even so, I did not grow up and pass my boyhood here. It was far away in the country of the Arabs that I grew up. Long long ago I was a native of a certain country near Bida, and the name of our town was Kagara. My father was a tall light-skinned man whose craft was leather-working. My mother was a native of Fatika. Now when my mother was carrying me, my father died and left me an inheritance of six cows, three sheep, and his riding mare. At this time the mare was in foal. All these things were handed over to my mother, who was told to keep them until in God's good time she should give birth, for they were the property of her son, since this husband of hers had no other relatives to claim the inheritance.

So things went on until one day I was born, and I turned out to be a boy. Now when the naming day came round, my mother had one of my rams caught and slaughtered, and the name of 'Umar' was whispered in my ear. Time passed until, when I was two years old (that is, the time for weaning), my grandmother on my father's side took me to wean me.

I lived with her until the time came when my mother wanted to marry again.

Then my mother said to my grandmother, 'You know that apart from you, I have no relations in this town besides this boy, and now I want to marry. What is more, many suitors have come forward to press their suit, saying that I must marry the one that I like best. I have come to you for advice. So-and-so and so-and-so seek my hand, but up to now I have not made up my mind which one I like best. I want first to hear what you have to say. Among them is a certain courtier, especially close to the Chief, called Makau.'

When my grandmother heard the name of Makau among the suitors, she said, 'My daughter, indeed God has brought you great good fortune! When there is one with good eyesight, would you marry a blind man? If you ask my advice, you should marry none save Makau. I know that he is a modest man, who is in no way mean-minded, and certainly if you marry him your home will be a happy one.'

My mother accepted this advice. The next day the marriage ceremony was performed, and a day was appointed upon which she was to move into her husband's compound. When the time came my mother went to live in her own hut, and I remained with my grandmother. I lived happily with my grandmother, and then one day a fatal illness came upon her. When she realized that she was not to recover, she sent for my mother to warn her, saying: 'See now, I do not think that I shall rise again from this illness, so I want you to take this boy home with you, because I do not want to see him cry even a single tear. It would make me very unhappy to see that.' My mother replied, 'Very well.'

Shortly after we had left, my grandmother died. Many people assembled, prayers were said over her, and she was laid in her grave.

When this was all over, I was living comfortably with my mother in Makau's compound, when one day the Chief had all his courtiers summoned. When they had assembled he said to them, 'The reason I have summoned you is this. I want you to make ready, and set out on a raid on my behalf to Gwari country. I am in dire need, and therefore I want you to make haste to set out, in the hope that you will return quickly.'

When the courtiers heard what the Chief had to say, they all went mad with joy. They were delighted, saying, 'Just give us half a chance, and we'll be off!' The reason for their delight was because, as you know, on a raid they would gain many cattle, and slaves as well. And then when they returned, the Chief would give them a part of everything which they had won. Thus if a man were to capture three slaves, the Chief would take two of them, and he would be allowed to keep one.

The reason for this raid that the Chief was planning, was that he wanted to obtain some slaves. Some he would put with his own, and send to Kano so that clothes and saddlery might be bought and sent back to him, while others he would send to Bida in order to procure muskets.

Among the horsemen whom the Chief had appointed as raiders was Makau. When the time came for their departure, after the Chief had sought an auspicious hour from a certain *malam*. Makau came into his compound and gathered his family together. He said to them, 'Now you know that I am going on a raid to Gwari country, and I do not know when I shall return. Whether I shall be killed there, God knows best. For this reason I want to bid you all farewell, and I want you to forgive me for all that I have done to you, for any man in this world, if you live with him, some day you are bound to cause him unhappiness.'

His family all spoke up together. 'By God, you have never done anything to make us unhappy. We wish you a safe journey, and a safe return.' Thereupon all of us burst out crying, so that none of us could hear the other!

The raiders all began to make ready, and in the early dawn they set out and made for the interior of Gwari country. They continued until they reached a small pagan village on a rocky stronghold in the forest. On their arrival in this place, they all dismounted from their horses, and lay down at the foot of some thick shady trees, where no-one could see them. At this season the rains had begun to set in, and all the farmers were about to clear their farms. Now there was no way that these pagans could sow a crop sufficient to feed them for a whole year, so they had to come out of their towns and come down to the low ground to lay out their farms in the plain. Despite this however, they were not able to tend their farms properly, for fear of raiders.

When the raiders reached the village they hid on the edge of the farms. Early in the morning, just before the time of prayer, the pagans began to come out from their villages, making for their farms. The raiders crouched silently, watching everything that they were doing. They held back until all the people had come out. Then, after they had settled down to work, thinking that nothing would happen to them, the raiders fell upon them all at once, and seized men and women, and even small children. Before the pagans had realized what was happening, the raiders had already done the damage. At once other pagans began to sally forth, preparing to fight to wrest back their brothers who had been captured. Af! Before they were ready, the raiders were far away. They started to follow them, but they had no chance of catching them. Those in front got clean away, leaving their pursuers far behind.

When the raiders saw that they had escaped, they took to the high road, for, as you know, they would not have followed the high road in the first place, lest the pagans should catch up with them. Then, when they got on to the high road they made haste, each saying to his companion, 'Come on, come on.' They kept on going until, by God's grace, they reached home safely. When they entered the town each one made straight for the palace, bringing with him his booty from the raid. All of them had at least two slaves, and there were some with three slaves, and even some with four. Each of them presented before the Chief that which he had obtained. Except for Makau. On his return, he had not gone by way of the palace, but had gone straight to his own compound. But this was not with any deceitful intent.

When everybody was present, each one handed over what he had brought. Then the Chief said, 'Where is Makau? Was he perhaps killed out there, and you are hiding it from me?'

The whole company answered together, 'Oh no, God save your Majesty, but you know what men are like. As for us, we kept quiet right from the start, when we saw he was your favourite, so as to see how it would all turn out between you. For we well know that anyone who is trusted, and betrays the trust, God will punish him, let alone in a case such as that of you and Makau, to whom you have entrusted everything that you possessed. Let us now skin the monkey for you, right down to its tail! In this whole town you will never find one who betrays your trust like this Makau. Why, it's Makau who shames you by revealing all your secrets to the common people, who you see, are giving themselves airs now. Why, there is never a secret that you tell him that some of them don't hear about. You know, from the time that we set out on this raid until we returned, this fellow never ceased to abuse you, to such an extent that Sarkin Zagi became angry and drew his sword, intending to strike off his head, until the Barde had to bid him hold his hand. The reason that you do not see him here now is that he gone by way of his own compound, in order to hide some of the slaves which he has acquired, for he captured four, two young girls and two boys, but one of them is almost grown up. But of course, we don't know, let's just wait and see what he is going to bring.'

When the Chief heard their words he said, 'So that's it, Makau has done well!'

After a little while Makau approached with the two young slaves whom he had captured, entirely unaware of what his fellow courtiers were plotting against him. Now these two slaves which he had brought were all that he had ever obtained, and the story that he had captured four slaves was a fabrication of his enemies. As Makau approached the gate of the palace, he saw from a distance the Chief seated outside, holding court. When the courtiers saw him they began to say, 'Aha, there's Makau coming with only two slaves, so he's hidden the other two, has he?' When Makau reached the Chief he prostrated himself in greeting, but the Chief did not reply. In the whole company there was not one who said as much as a single word to him. Each one just kept staring at him, and his rivals were overjoyed, as though they had been given hump to roast!

After a little while the Chief said, 'Makau, is it only now that you have arrived?' He replied. 'No, God save your

Majesty, I went by way of my compound, so as to tether my horse and change my clothes, before coming to your presence.'

The Chief said, 'I see, and how many slaves did you get?'

Makau said, 'Two.'

The Chief said, 'Right. Are you sure you only got two? Do you agree that if I investigate and find that it was not two that you got, I should do to you whatever I like?'

Makau said, 'Most certainly, I agree.'

When they had finished this exchange, the Chief called the Sarkin Zagi and asked him, 'How many slaves is it that Makau brought back from the raid?'

Now all along the Sarkin Zagi had been waiting eagerly for this to happen, and he said, 'Four slaves, but he only entered the city with two, because he sold the other two on the road to a caravan of Kano people who were going to fetch locust-bean cake for Bauci.'

The Chief said, 'So, do you hear that, Makau?'

Makau replied, 'God save your Majesty, I have nothing more to say, for these people have already told so many lies that there is nothing more that I can tell you that you will believe.'

Then the Chief became enraged, and sent the courtiers off and gave them permission to go and ransack Makau's compound, ordering them not to leave him a single thing, even if only a sleeping mat. The courtiers went and stripped his compound to the ground, even the grass with which the roofs of the huts were thatched, all was stripped. He had some cattle in a little village near the town, and there and then someone was sent to fetch them. Now when they went to bring back these cattle of Makau's, they included mine, which my father had left me as an inheritance, and also my sheep, and my mare, and her foal. After they had completely finished this pillage they gathered up the property and took it to the Chief.

When it was brought Makau rose and said to the Chief, 'God save your Majesty, I beg you, among this property there are some things which do not belong to me, such as this mare and her foal, the sheep, and some cattle. These things belong to a certain boy, an orphan, whose mother I married. I beg you, take out this orphan's property and restore it to him.'

On hearing this the courtiers all spoke at once, 'Aha, you hear, there he goes with those lies of his again! How do you come to be making out that you've got an orphan's property in your keeping? May God save your Majesty, he's lying. This property of the orphan that he's talking about, it's not in his keeping at all, it's in the keeping of the boy's mother and she knows what she has done with it.' (At this time I was a small boy, hardly able to talk properly, much less could I understand what was happening. When they ransacked the compound, all I knew was that my parents were weeping.)

Then and there, without making any inquiries at all, the Chief accepted what the courtiers told him. After it was finished, he said to Makau, 'So, you see, this is the reward which you get from God for having betrayed my trust, after I had trusted you. Now I have nothing more to say to you; what has been done to you is sufficient. After this, as long as I am Chief in this town, I will not permit you to remain in it. And so I shall banish you to somewhere far away, not under my jurisdiction. However, I will not forbid you to take your family with you. Any one of your wives, if she loves you, let her follow you, and you can go together. But if she does not love you, then you must leave her behind.'

Makau said, 'God save your Majesty. I hear and I obey. But I beg you, in the majesty of your kingship, allow me a few days here to obtain certain provision to eat on the road, for as you know, I am now going to an unfamiliar place.'

The Chief raised his head for a time. Then he answered Makau, saying that he agreed, but that he would give him four days only, to make ready for his exile.

Makau thanked him, got up, came back to his compound, and gathered all his family together, old and young, male and female, and said to us, 'Well now, you have seen how God has decreed that this thing should happen to me. The Chief has said that I must leave his country, but he will allow me to take with me any wife who wishes to follow me, and in addition he has said that I must leave this town within four days. Now what I want to say is this, if any woman among you is sure in her heart that she can bear to follow me, well and good, let her come.'

His whole family burst into tears together, saying, 'By God, we swear that even if it be no other country on earth that you are bound for, even if it be the next world, if it is possible to accompany you there, we shall accompany you.'

Makau asked us thrice, according to the Law, but not one of us changed his mind.

From Shaihu Umar, by Alhaji Sir Abubakar Balewa, Longmans, Green and Co., Ltd., 1967.

The Old Man of Usumbura and His Misery

by Taban Lo Liyong

Taban Lo Liyong was born in Uganda about 1939. He left home to study writing at the Writer's Workshop of the University of Iowa, where he was the first African to receive a Master of Fine Arts degree. On his return to Africa, he began writing short stories that combined the elements of the traditional storytelling style of the Luo and Masai tribes with a keen sense of humour and tragedy. In addition to short stories and poems, he has written essays concerning the role of the creative artist in Africa.

His work has been collected in two anthologies, *Fixions and Other Stories* and *Eating Chiefs*. In *The Old Man of Usumbura and His Misery* he has created an African myth based on the hidden evil in mankind and the perils of curiosity.

There was an old man of Usumbura who was very rich. This old man of Usumbura. He was so rich he had eight thousand

The Old Man of Usumbura and His Misery 73

cows. This rich old man of Usumbura. With these cows he married for himself sixty-five wives. The old man of Usumbura. He was so healthy that he had three hundred children from these wives. Our healthy man of Usumbura. He was so happy and successful that with industry his wealth increased manifoldly. This happy successful and industrious man of Usumbura. He and all the members of his family were so lucky none of them ever felt sick. These lucky people of Usumbura. All his life he had never known the pangs of sorrow or grief. This lucky Usumburan.

There was another old man of Kigali who was very poor. This old man of Kigali. He was thoroughly sunk in misery. This miserable man of Kigali. His eyes were always red with weeping. The eyes of the man of Kigali. He was rich once. This previously rich man of Kigali. But he had lost all his worldly goods to the last bit. This erstwhile rich man of Kigali. He had not even a wife left him now. This old man of Kigali. Not even a child was left to console him in his old age and poverty. This bereft man of Kigali. All day long he mourned for his lost cows. This old man of Kigali. He also wept for his dead wives. This single man of Kigali. He wept all night for his dead children. This mourning old man of Kigali. He always cried, 'Oh, my misery! Oh, my misery!' This miserable old man.

The rich, happy old man of Usumbura and the poor, miserable old man of Kigali were friends. These old men of Usumbura and Kigali.

One day the rich old man of Usumbura went on a journey. This rich old man of Usumbura. He went to Kigali. This rich man of Usumbura. He went to visit his poor friend. This rich man of Usumbura. When he arrived at Kigali he was struck by his friend's cry of 'Oh, my misery' and became sympathetic. This happy man of Usumbura. He asked to be shown the nature of misery. This healthy man of Usumbura. The miserable man of Kigali tried to discourage him. This adventurous old man of Usumbura. But he would hear none of that. This happy healthy rich old man of Usumbura. He seemed to have been so bored with his constantly happy life that he needed a change. This lucky man of Usumbura. Any kind of a change would be better than that drab happy life. That life of this unmiserable man of Usumbura. At last the miserable old man of Kigali consented to give a slice of misery to his happy friend from Usumbura. These old friends of Kigali and Usumbura.

They appointed a date when misery would be conveyed from Kigali to Usumbura. These old men of Kigali and Usumbura. The rich man's sons were to come and convey misery from Kigali to Usumbura. These lucky sons of Usumbura. They were to transport misery from the poor man's home to their rich father's home. These happy obedient sons of Usumbura.

On the day appointed all the one hundred and fifty-one sons started off early for Kigali. These fat children of Usumbura. They ran part of the way. These expectant sons of Usumbura. Instead of taking two days to reach Kigali they did it in one day. These impatient and obedient sons of Usumbura. It was evening when they reached Kigali. These heirs of Usumbura. They rested a while but ate nothing in Kigali. These worthy agents of fate. In the evening they insisted they be given misery straightaway to take home to Usumbura. These playful sons of Usumbura. The old man of Kigali suggested they wait till the following morning. This unknown old man of Kigali. But as would be expected these hot-headed sons of Usumbura would not like a delay. These children full of great expectations. The old man of Kigali thought the time had come to give them misery. And he was right, this old man of Kigali.

The old man of Kigali gave them a very large straw bundle. This large straw bundle. This bundle was tightly tied with ropes. The tightly tied bundle. It contained the very misery so greatly desired by the old rich Usumbura man. This loved misery. It contained the misery so desired by the hundred and fifty-one children. This loved misery.

The old man of Kigali gave the sons of Usumbura a few orders. This knowing man of Kigali. The children were never to tamper with the luggage. They were to carry it right before their father. These inquisitive children. The children shouted for joy. These live children of Usumbura. They managed in their own way to convey this heavy burden a

The Old Man of Usumbura and His Misery   75

few steps at a time. Nothing was heavier to each of them than this pregnant egg. The incurious Usumburans.

When the bundle had left Kigali the old man started to smile. This prescient man of Kigali.

Midway between Kigali and Usumbura these boys stopped. These obedient children of Usumbura. Some of them said they were tired. These lively children of Usumbura. Others thought they needed to enjoy a bit of the sunset. These observant children of Usumbura. A few thought a little rest was in order. These restless children of Usumbura. One admitted he really needed a relaxation. These playful children of Usumbura. One said the rope looked green. These children who can see green at night. One thought the rope had surely loosened since they had left Kigali. One wagered he would loosen one, just one of the knots. These indefatigable children of Usumbura. One said he was tickled by misery on the side next to him. These sensible children of Usumbura. One boy exhibited with triumph a rope unloosened. These active children of Usumbura. The elder ordered there be no tampering with misery. This orderly elder son. But another thought only blind people carry what they cannot see. These seeing children of Usumbura. So an argument grew up between the children who wanted to see misery before it reached their father and those who wanted their father to see misery first. These factious children. While the argument was in progress some children stayed unconcerned. These apathetic and reflective children. But a few boys were busy with their nimble hands. These constant active few.

The bundle became smaller and smaller as the argument became louder and louder. This bundle and strife. Nothing substantial could be seen yet from the bundle although brother was already abusing brother. This cause of strife. Blows started to rain on brothers' heads. These headbreaking blows. At last a handful of the luggage remained. That fatal unknown. Curiosity brought brothers together to see this famed thing. The curiosity that killed the cat. They squeezed together, they held their breaths, they were ready to see, they were all attention. These humans.

When the bundle was opened, nothing was seen. The

cheated sights. Only a little whirring sound was heard. The noise that has no path. It sounded like a mosquito. This child of the egg.

Now that there was no more misery to carry home, what were these boys to carry home to their father? These obedient boys of Usumbura. One brother's hands were already striking another for having opened the bundle. These useful hands we have. Another hit another on the head, another smote another, another slew another, another clubbed another, another speared another, another strangled another, another castrated another, another drank another's blood. These killers of their own brothers. Now only fifty brothers remained in the internecine war. These brother-killing brothers. Three minutes later we see only three blood-intoxicated brothers. These committed brothers. Two brothers have ganged up on a brother. The unhappy company. The last round ends with brother killing brother. Oh, the fatal end. Death, you have reaped a rich harvest. Death that levels all. Alas, who will inform the rich man of Usumbura? That rich, happy, wealthy, unmiserable old man of Usumbura.

But one boy remained alive. This unlucky boy of Usumbura. He had always been a coward. This life-preserving son of his mother. He had hidden away during the life-destroying brotherly exercises. That fatal exercise. He became the messenger of misery to his father. Oh, the fatal messenger that should never arrive. Out of breath with sorrow and running, he approached his expectant father with the news. This sorrow-filled son of his beaming father. The father anticipated an advance information on the approaching misery. This happy father of Usumbura. He asked how near misery was. This impatient father of Usumbura. He repeated the question with anger. This father who can't even wait for his son to regain his breath. He struck the son once for the delay. This father who had never known how to strike a blow. But only good news comes out pat. This bad news which demands a cautious framing. The son started to sob, more from internal blows. This vessel of deaths. At last he said misery had escaped. The misery that travels in the air. The old man of Usumbura was so mad he struck his son dead instantly. This happy, rich, healthy, misery-less old man of Usumbura.

The rich, happy, healthy, worry-less old man of Usumbura has now killed his son. This father who does not know misery. The wife whose son was struck dead started to mourn. In this home that has never known mourning. Other wives realized that she had deserved such a treatment for a long time past. Oh, human wisdom that always condemns those who are afflicted. This mother's wrong deeds consist of insolence. Oh, the home that never knew insolence. And her son was said to have been disrespectful to their worthy husband. Oh, the love that is intensified by the degradation of others. He was the only black sheep in this snow-white home. Give a dog a name and you hang him. His mother left the home of the rich old man that very night. The darkest of nights. She did not carry her son's corpse with her. The lifeless luggage. It was her share of misery she took along with her. Oh, misery that curiosity brings.

The old man of Usumbura set out that very night to find his other hundred and forty-nine sons. These all-virtuous sons. He took along with him his fifty-five wives. The wives that love their husband and never do wrong. Husband and wives went to find sons and misery. Oh, obsessions that are so dear to the hearts.

On the way the smell of new blood tickled their noses. Smell that travels in the wind. They became wild. These good people. Soon they stepped on cadaver instead of earth. Oh, organic flesh and earth. They kissed their lifeless sons because there was nothing else to do. These virtuous sons and wives. They had no more stomach for misery. These misery-filled parents.

They abandoned their happy husband to his fate and went off to their several parents' homes. These good wives of Usumbura. They took with them all their daughters and share of wealth. These unlike-the-other-wife wives.

At last the old man was left to bear his misery alone. The old man who had wanted so much to see misery. He sang a song called 'Oh, my misery! Oh, my misery!' This rich, healthy, happy, misery-less old man of Usumbura.

Tekayo

by Grace Ogot

Grace Ogot is one of the most sensitive woman writers in Africa. Born in Nyanza province, Kenya, in 1930, she trained as a general nurse and midwife in Uganda and England. She helped to set up students' health services at Makerere University College and worked as a community development officer in Nyanza. Her talent for writing led her to a job as scriptwriter for the British Broadcasting Company and subsequently as public relations officer for an international airline.

Mrs Ogot has had many short stories published, and one novel, *The Promised Land*. Her stories reflect her rich experiences with many different kinds of people, and the conflicts which naturally arise between the generations and between superstition and modern scientific knowledge.

The period of short rains was just starting in a semi-arid part of the Sudan. The early morning mist had cleared, and faint blue smoke rose from the ground as the hot sun touched the surface of the wet earth.

'People in the underworld are cooking.
People in the underworld are cooking!'

The children shouted, as they pelted one another with wet sand.

'Come on, Opija,' Tekayo shouted to his son. 'Give me a hand, I must get the cows to the river before it is too hot.'

Opija hit his younger brother with his last handful of sand, and then ran to help his father. The cows were soon out of the village and Tekayo picked up the leather pouch containing his lunch and followed them.

They had not gone far from home when Tekayo saw an

eagle flying above his head with a large piece of meat in its claws. The eagle was flying low searching for a suitable spot to have its meal. Tekayo promptly threw his stick at the bird. He hit the meat and it dropped to the ground. It was a large piece of liver, and fresh blood was still oozing from it. Tekayo nearly threw the meat away, but he changed his mind. What was the use of robbing the eagle of its food only to throw it away? The meat looked good: it would supplement his vegetable lunch wonderfully. He wrapped the meat in a leaf and pushed it into his pouch.

They reached a place where there was plenty of grass. Tekayo allowed the cows to graze while he sat under an *ober* tree watching the sky. It was not yet lunch time, but Tekayo could not wait. The desire to taste that meat was burning within him. He took out the meat and roasted it on a log fire under the *ober* tree. When the meat was cooked he ate it greedily with millet bread which his wife had made the previous night.

'My! What delicious meat,' Tekayo exclaimed. He licked the fat juice that stained his fingers, and longed for a little more. He threw away the bitter herbs that were the rest of his lunch. The meat was so good, and the herbs would merely spoil its taste.

The sun was getting very hot, but the cows showed no desire to go to the river to drink. One by one they lay down in the shade, chewing the cud. Tekayo also became overpowered by the afternoon heat. He rested against the trunk and slept.

While asleep, Tekayo had a dream. He was sitting before a log fire roasting a large piece of liver like the one he had eaten earlier. His mouth watered as he watched rich fat from the roasting meat dropping into the fire. He could not wait, and although the meat was not completely done, he removed it from the fire and cut it up with his hunting knife. But just as he was about to take the first bite, he woke up.

Tekayo looked around him, wondering what had happened to the meat! Could it be that he was dreaming? 'No, no, no,' he cried. 'It was too vivid to be a dream!' He sat upright and had another look around, as if by some miracle he might see a piece of liver roasting on the log fire beside him. But there was nothing. All he saw were large roots of the old tree protruding above the earth's surface like sweet potatoes in the sandy soil.

The cattle had wandered a long way off. Tekayo got up and followed them. They reached the river bank, and the thirsty cows ran to the river. While the cows drank, Tekayo sat on a white stone cooling his feet and gazing lazily at the swollen river as it flowed mightily towards the plain.

Beyond the river stood the great 'Ghost Jungle.' A strong desire for the rich meat came back to Tekayo, and he whispered. 'The animal with that delicious liver must surely be in that jungle.' He sat there for a while, thinking. The temptation to start hunting for the animal nagged him. But he managed to suppress it. The afternoon was far spent and they were a long way from home.

The next morning Tekayo left home earlier than usual. When his wife begged him to wait for his lunch, he refused. He hurried from home, taking his hunting spears with him.

Tekayo made it impossible for the cows to graze. He rushed them along, lashing at any cow that lingered in one spot for long. They reached the edge of the 'Ghost Jungle' and there he left the cows grazing unattended.

Tekayo could not see any path or track leading into the 'Ghost Jungle.' The whole place was a mass of thick bush and long grass covered with the morning dew. And except for the sounds of mating birds, there was a weird silence in the jungle that frightened him. But the vehement desire within him blindly drove him on, through the thick wet grass.

After walking for some time, he stood and listened. Something was racing towards him. He turned around to look, and sure enough a big impala was running frantically towards him. Warm blood rushed through Tekayo's body, and he raised his spear to kill the animal. But the spear never landed. He came face to face with a big leopardess that was chasing the impala. The leopardess roared at Tekayo several times challenging him, as it were, to a duel. But Tekayo looked away, clutching the spear in his trembling hand. There was no one to fight and the beast went away after her prey.

'What a bad start,' Tekayo said slowly and quietly when

his heart beat normally again. 'That wild cat will not leave me alone now.'

He started to walk back towards the plain, following the track he had made. The roaring leopardess had taken the life out of him.

He saw another track that cut across the forest. He hesitated a little, and then decided to follow it, leaving his own. The track got bigger and bigger, and without any warning Tekayo suddenly came upon a baby wildebeeste which was following a large flock grazing at the foot of a hill. He killed it without any difficulty. He skinned the animal and extracted its liver, leaving the rest of the carcass there.

Tekayo returned to the herd, and he sat down to roast the meat on a log fire. When the meat was cooked he took a bite and chewed it hurriedly. But he did not swallow it: he spat it all out! The liver was as bitter as the strong green herbs given to constipated children. The back of his tongue was stinging as if it had been burned. Tekayo threw the rest of the meat away and took his cows home.

He arrived home tired and disappointed; and when his young wife set food before him, he refused to eat. He pretended that he had a stomach-ache and did not feel like eating. That night Tekayo was depressed and in low spirits. He did not even desire his young wife who slept by his side. At dawn the young wife returned to her hut disappointed, wondering why the old man had not desired her.

The doors of all the huts were still closed when Tekayo looked out through his door. A cold east wind hit his face, and he quickly shut himself in again.

It was getting rather late and the calves were calling. But it was pouring with rain so much that he could not start milking. He sat on the hard bed looking at the dead ashes in the fire-place. He longed to get out to start hunting.

When the rain stopped, Tekayo milked the cows in a great hurry. Then he picked up the lunch that had been left near his hut for him, and left the village. His disappointed wife of the previous night watched him till he disappeared at the gate.

When he reached the 'Ghost Jungle,' it was drizzling again. The forest looked so lonely and wet. He left the cows grazing as usual, and entered the bush, stealing his way through the dripping leaves. He turned to the left to avoid the thick part of the jungle. Luck was with him. He spotted a family of antelope grazing not far from him. He crawled on his knees till he was quite close to them, and then threw his spear killing one animal instantly. After skinning it, he extracted its liver, and also took some delicate parts for the family.

When he sat down under the tree to roast the meat, Tekayo was quite sure that he had been successful. But when he tasted the meat, he shook his head. The meat was tender, but it was not what he was looking for.

They reached the river bank. The cows continued to graze after drinking, and Tekayo, without realizing it, wandered a long way from his herd, still determined to discover the owner of that wonderful liver. When he suddenly looked round, the herd was nowhere to be seen. The sun was sinking behind Mount Pajulu, and Tekayo started to run, looking for his cows.

The cows, heavy with milk, had gone home without Tekayo. For one day when Tekayo's children got lost in the forest, the cows had gone home without them, following the old track they knew well. On that day the whole village came out in search of the children in fear that the wild animals might harm them.

It was getting dark when Tekayo arrived home. They started to milk and Odipo remarked, 'Why, Father, you are late coming home today.'

'It is true,' replied Tekayo thoughtfully. 'See that black bull there? He went to another herd across the river. I didn't miss him until it was time to come home. One of these days, we shall have to castrate him – he is such a nuisance.'

They milked in silence until one of the little girls came to fetch some milk for preparing vegetables.

At supper time the male members of the family sat around the log fire waiting and talking. One by one, baskets of millet meal and earthen dishes of meat and vegetables arrived from different huts. There was fish, dried meat, fried white ants, and herbs. A little food was thrown to the ground, to the ancestors, and then they started eating. They compared and contrasted the delicious-ness of the various dishes they were having. But Tekayo kept quiet. All the food he tasted that evening was bitter as bile.

When the meal was over, the adults told stories of war and the clans to the children, who listened attentively. But Tekayo was not with them: he was not listening. He watched the smoky clouds as they raced across the sky.

'Behind those clouds, behind those clouds, rests Okenyu, my great-grandfather. Please! Please!' Tekayo beseeched him. 'Please, Father, take this longing away from me. Give me back my manhood that I may desire my wives. For what is a man without this desire!'

A large cloud covered the moon giving the earth temporary darkness. Tears stung Tekayo's eyes, and he dismissed the family to sleep. As he entered his own hut, a woman was throwing small logs on the fire.

He offered many secret prayers to the departed spirits, but the craving for the mysterious liver never left him. Day after day he left home in the morning, taking his cows with him. And on reaching the jungle, he left them unattended while he hunted. The rough and disappointed life that he led soon became apparent to the family. He suddenly became old and disinterested in life. He had nothing to tell his sons around the evening fire, and he did not desire his wives. The sons of Tekayo went to Lakech and told her, 'Mother, speak to Father – he is sick. He does not talk to us, and he does not eat. We don't know how to approach him.'

Though Lakech had passed the age of child-bearing and no longer went to Tekayo's hut at night, she was his first wife, and he loved her. She therefore went and asked him, 'Man, what ails you?' Tekayo looked at Lakech, but he could not look into her eyes. He looked at her long neck, and instead of answering her question he asked her, 'Would you like to get free from those heavy brass rings around your neck?'

'Why?' Lakech replied, surprised.

'Because they look so tight.'

'But they are not tight,' Lakech said softly. 'I would feel naked without them.'

And Tekayo looked away from his wife. He was longing to tell Lakech everything, and to share with her this maddening craving that was tearing his body to pieces. But he checked himself. Lakech must not know: she would not understand. Then he lied to her.

'It is my old indigestion. I have had it for weeks now. It will soon pass.'

A mocking smile played on Lakech's lips, and Tekayo knew that she was not convinced. Some visitors arrived, and Lakech left her husband.

Tekayo hunted for many months, but he did not succeed in finding the animal with the delicious liver.

One night, as he lay awake, he asked himself where else he could hunt. And what animal would he be looking for? He had killed all the different animals in the 'Ghost Jungle.' He had risked his life when he killed and ate the liver of a lion, a leopard and a hyena, all of which were tabooed by his clan.

A little sleep came to Tekayo's heavy eyes and he was grateful. But then Apii stood beside his bed calling: 'Grandpa, Grandpa, it is me.' Tekayo sat up, but the little girl was not there. He went back to sleep again. And Apii was there calling him: 'Can't you hear me, Grandpa?'

Tekayo woke up a second time, but nobody was there. He lay down without closing his eyes. Again the child's fingers touched his drooping hand, and the playful voice of a child tickled the skin of the old man. Tekayo sat up a third time, and looked round the room. But he was alone. The cock crew a third time, and it was morning.

And Lakech died without knowing her husband's secret, and was buried in the middle of the village, being the first wife. Tekayo sat at his wife's grave morning and evening for a long time, and his grief for her appeased his hunger for the unknown animal's liver. He wept, but peacefully, as if his craving for the liver was buried with his wife.

It was during this time of grief that Tekayo decided never to go hunting again. He sat at home and looked after his many grandchildren, while the younger members of the family went out to work daily in the fields.

And then one day as Tekayo sat warming himself in the

early morning sun near the granary, he felt slightly sick from the smell of grain sprouting inside the dark store. The shouting and singing of his grandchildren attracted his attention. As he watched them playing, the craving for the liver of the unknown animal returned powerfully to him.

Now among the children playing was a pretty little girl called Apii, the daughter of Tekayo's eldest son. Tekayo sent the other children away to play, and as they were going, he called Apii and told her, 'Come my little one, run to your mother's hut and bring me a calabash of water.'

Apii ran to her mother's hut to get water for her grandfather. And while she was fumbling in a dark corner of the house looking for a clean calabash, strong hands gripped her neck and strangled her. She gave a weak cry as she struggled for the breath of life. But it was too much for her. Her eyes closed in everlasting sleep, never to see the beauty of the shining moon again.

The limp body of the child slipped from Tekayo's hands and fell on the floor with a thud. He looked at the body at his feet and felt sick and faint. His ears were buzzing. He picked up the body, and as he staggered out with it, the air seemed black, and the birds of the air screamed ominously at him. But Tekayo had to eat his meal. He buried the body of Apii in a nearby anthill in a shallow grave.

The other children were still playing in the field when Tekayo returned with the liver in his bag. He roasted it in his hut hastily and ate it greedily. And alas! It was what he had been looking for for many years. He sat lazily resting his back on the granary, belching and picking his teeth. The hungry children, back from their play in the fields, sat in the shade eating sweet potatoes and drinking sour milk.

The older people came back in the evening, and the children ran to meet their parents. But Apii was not amongst them. In great desperation they asked the grandfather about the child. But Tekayo replied, 'Ask the children – they should know where Apii is. They were playing together in the fields.'

It was already pitch dark. Apii's younger brothers and sisters sat in front of the fire weeping with their mother. It was then that they remembered their grandfather sending

Apii to fetch water for him. The desperate parents repeated this information to the old man, asking him if Apii had brought water for him that morning.

'She did,' Tekayo replied, 'and then ran away after the others. I watched her go with my own eyes. When they came back, I was asleep.'

The grief-stricken family sat near the fire-place, their heads in their hands. They neither ate nor drank. Outside the little crickets sang in chorus as if they had a secret to tell.

For many days Apii's parents looked for their child, searching every corner and every nook. But there was no trace of her. Apii was gone. Months went by, and people talked no more about the disappearance of Apii. Only her mother thought of her. She did not lose hope of finding her child alive one day.

Tekayo forgot his deed. And when he killed a second child in the same way to satisfy his savage appetite, he was not even conscious of what he was doing. And when the worried parents asked the old man about the child, Tekayo wept saying, 'How could I know? The children play out in the fields – I stay here at home.'

It was after this that Tekayo's sons said among themselves, 'Who steals our children? Which animal can it be? Could it be a hyena? Or a leopard? But these animals only hunt at night. Could it be an eagle, because it hunts during the day? But no! Father would have seen the eagle – he would have heard the child screaming.' After some thought, Aganda told his brother, 'Perhaps it is a malicious animal brought upon us by the evil spirits.'

'Then my father is too old to watch the children,' put in Osogo. 'Yes, Father is too old, he is in danger,' the rest agreed.

And from that time onwards the sons kept watch secretly on the father and the children. They watched for many months, but nothing threatened the man and the children.

The sons were almost giving up the watch. But one day when it was the turn of Apii's father to keep watch, he saw Tekayo sending away the children to play in the field – all except one. He sent this child to fetch him a pipe from his hut. As the child ran to the hut, Tekayo followed him. He clasped the frightened child and dragged him towards the fire-place. As Tekayo was struggling with the child, a heavy blow landed on his old back. He turned round sharply, his hands still holding the child's neck. He was facing Aganda, his eldest son. The child broke loose from the limp hands of Tekayo and grabbed Aganda's knees as if he had just escaped from the teeth of a crocodile. 'Father!' Aganda shouted.

Seeing that the child was not hurt, Aganda pushed him aside saying, 'Go to your mother's hut and lie down.'

He then got hold of the old man and dragged him towards the little windowless hut built for goats and sheep. As he was being dragged away, the old man kept on crying, '*Atimo ang'o? Atimo ang'o?* (What have I done? What have I done?)

Aganda pushed the old man into the little hut and barred the door behind him, as you would to the animals. He went to the child, who was still sobbing.

The rest of the family returned from the fields, and when Apii's father broke the news to them, they were appalled. The family wore mourning garments and went without food.

'Tho! Tho!' they spat towards the sun which, although setting on them, was rising on the ancestors.

'Great-grandfathers, cleanse us,' they all cried.

And they lit the biggest fire that had ever been lit in that village. Tekayo's eldest son took the old greasy drum hanging above the fire-place in his father's hut and beat it. The drum throbbed out sorrowful tunes to warn the clan that there was sad news in Tekayo's home. The people who heard the drum left whatever they were doing and ran to Tekayo's village following the sound of the drum. Within a short time the village was teeming with anxious-looking relatives.

'What news? What news?' they asked in trembling voices.
'And where is Tekayo?' another old man asked.
'Is he in good health?' asked another.
There was confusion and panic.
'Death of death, who will give us medicine for death? Death knocks at your door, and before you can tell him to

come in, he is in the house with you.'

'Listen!' Someone touched the old woman who was mourning about death. Aganda spoke to the people.

'Men of my clan. We have not called you here for nothing. Listen to me and let our sorrow be yours. Weep with up! For several months we have been losing our children when we go to work on the fields. Apii, my own child, was the first one to disappear.' Sobbing broke out among the women at the mention of the children's names.

'My people,' Aganda continued, 'the children in this clan get sick and die. But ours disappear unburied. It was our idea to keep watch over our children that we may catch whoever steals them. For months we have been watching secretly. We were almost giving up because we thought it was probably the wrath of our ancestors that was upon us. But today I caught him.'

'What man? What man?' the people demanded angrily.

'And from what clan is he?' others asked.

'We must declare war on his clan, we must we must!'

Aganda stopped for a while, and told them in a quavering voice, 'The man is in that little hut. The man is no one else but my father.'

'*Mayo!*' the women shouted. There was a scuffle and the women and children screamed as if Tekayo was around the fire, and they were afraid of him. But the men kept quiet.

When the commotion died down, an old man asked, 'Do you speak the truth, man?'

The son nodded. Men and women now shouted, 'Where is the man? Kill him! He is not one of us. He is not one of us. He is an animal!'

There was nothing said outside that Tekayo did not hear. And there in the hut the children he had killed haunted him. He laid his head on the rough wall of the hut and wept.

Outside the hut the angry villagers continued with their demand, shouting, 'Stone him now! Stone him now! Let his blood be upon his own head!'

But one of the old men got up and calmed the people.

'We cannot stone him now. It is the custom of the clan that a wicked man should be stoned in broad daylight, outside the village. We cannot depart from this custom.'

'Stone me now, stone me now,' Tekayo whispered. 'Take me quickly from this torture and shame. Let me die and be finished with.'

Tekayo knew by the angry shouting of the men and the shrill cries of frightened women and children that he was banished from society, nay, from life itself. He fumbled in his leather bag suspended around his waist to find his hunting knife, but it was not there. It had been taken away from him.

The muttering and shouting continued outside. There was weeping too. But Tekayo was now hearing them from afar as if a powerful wave were carrying him further and further away from his people.

At dawn the villagers got up from the fireplace to gather stones from nearby fields. The sun was not up yet, but it was just light enough to see. Everyone in the clan must throw a stone at the murderer. It was bad not to throw a stone, for it was claimed that the murderer's wicked spirit would rest upon the man who did not help to drive him away.

When the first rays of the sun appeared, the villagers had gathered enough stones to cover several bodies. They returned to the village to fetch Tekayo from the hut, and to lead him to his own garden outside the village. They surrounded the hut and stood in silence, waiting to jeer and spit at him when he came out.

Aganda and three old men tore the papyrus door open and called Tekayo to come out. But there was no reply. They rushed into the hut to drag him out to the people who were now demanding. 'Come out, come out!'

At first it was too dark to see. But soon their eyes got used to the darkness. Then they saw the body of Tekayo, hanged on a short rope that he had unwound from the thatched roof.

The men came out shaking their heads. The crowd peered into the hut in turn until all of them had seen the dangling body of Tekayo – the man they were preparing to stone. No one spoke. Such a man, they knew, would have to be buried outside the village. They knew too that no newborn child would ever be named after him.

Chief Priest of Ulu

by Chinua Achebe

Chinua Achebe, born in 1930 in Eastern Nigeria, is the author of several novels about traditional Ibo society, spanning several generations and going back to the days of his grandfather. Although he includes the white man in his novels, the viewpoint is primarily African, and the characters in his books speak with the authentic voice of their African heritage.

One of his most memorable characters is the Chief Priest of Ulu in *Arrow of God*, a novel of Ibo life set in the thirties, well before independence. This story of the impact of colonialism on traditional African society won the British New Statesman novel award in 1965. Throughout the book, in scene after scene, the author builds a picture of Ibo society as the chief priest sees it.

Arrow of God is richly told, in the language of symbolism, full of proverbs, tribal wisdom, and humour. In one scene, the priest Ezeulu says, 'The white man is like hot soup, and we must take him slowly, slowly, from the edges of the bowl.' Even his caution is not enough to avoid the confrontation between old and new ways in the following episode involving his son Oduche and the sacred python.

The place where the Christians built their place of worship was not far from Ezeulu's compound. As he sat in his *obi* thinking of the Festival of the Pumpkin Leaves, he heard their bell: GOME, GOME, GOME, GOME, GOME. His mind turned from the festival to the new religion. He was not sure what to make of it. At first he had thought that since the white man had come with great power and conquest it was necessary that some people should learn the ways of his own deity. That was why he had agreed to send his son,

Oduche, to learn the new ritual. He also wanted him to learn the white man's wisdom, for Ezeulu knew from what he saw of Wintabota and the stories he heard about his people that the white man was very wise.

But now Ezeulu was becoming afraid that the new religion was like a leper. Allow him a handshake and he wants an embrace. Ezeulu had already spoken strongly to his son who was becoming more strange every day. Perhaps the time had come to bring him out again. But what would happen if, as many oracles prophesied, the white man had come to take over the land and rule? In such a case it would be wise to have a man of your family in his band. As he thought about these things Oduche came out from the inner compound wearing a white singlet and a towel which they had given him in the school. Nwafo came out with him, admiring his singlet. Oduche saluted his father and set out for the mission because it was Sunday morning. The bell continued ringing in its sad monotone.

Nwafo came back to the *obi* and asked his father whether he knew what the bell was saying. Ezeulu shook his head.

'It is saying: Leave your yam, leave your cocoyam and come to church. That is what Oduche says.'

'Yes,' said Ezeulu thoughtfully. 'It tells them to leave their yam and their cocoyam, does it? Then it is singing the song of extermination.'

They were interrupted by loud and confused talking inside the compound, and Nwafo ran out to see what it was. The voices were getting louder and Ezeulu who normally took no interest in women's shouting began to strain his ear. But Nwafo soon rushed back.

'Oduche's box is moving,' he said, out of breath with excitement. The tumult in the compound grew louder. As usual the voice of Ezeulu's daughter, Akueke, stood out above all others.

'What is called "Oduche's box is moving"?' he asked, rising with deliberate slowness to belie his curiosity.

'It is moving about the floor.'

'There is nothing that a man will not hear nowadays.' He went into his inner compound through the door at the back of his *obi*. Nwafo ran past him to the group of excited women outside his mother's hut. Akueke and Matefi did most of the talking. Nwafo's mother, Ugoye, was speechless. Now and again she rubbed her palms together and showed them to the sky.

Akueke turned to Ezeulu as soon as she saw him. 'Father, come and see what we are seeing. This new religion . . .'

'Shut your mouth,' said Ezeulu, who did not want anybody, least of all his own daughter, to question his wisdom in sending one of his sons to join the new religion.

The wooden box had been brought from the room where Oduche and Nwafo slept and placed in the central room of their mother's hut where people sat during the day and food was cooked.

The box, which was the only one of its kind in Ezeulu's compound, had a lock. Only people of the church had such boxes made for them by the mission carpenter and they were highly valued in Umuaro. Oduche's box was not actually moving; but it seemed to have something inside it struggling to be free. Ezeulu stood before it wondering what to do. Whatever was inside the box became more violent and actually moved the box around. Ezeulu waited for it to calm down a little, bent down and carried the box outside. The women and children scattered in all directions.

'Whether it be bad medicine or good one, I shall see it today,' he said as he carried the box at arm's length like a potent sacrifice. He did not pass through his *obi*, but took the door in the red-earth wall of his compound. His second son, Obika, who had just come in, followed him. Nwafo came closely behind Obika, and the women and children followed fearfully at a good distance. Ezeulu looked back and asked Obika to bring him a matchet. He took the box right outside his compound and finally put it down by the side of the common footpath. He looked back and saw Nwafo and the women and children.

'Every one of you go back to the house. The inquisitive monkey gets a bullet in the face.'

They moved back not into the compound but in front of the *obi*. Obika took a matchet to his father who thought for a little while and put the matchet aside and sent him for the spear used in digging up yams. The struggling inside the box was as fierce as ever. For a brief moment Ezeulu wondered whether the wisest thing was not to leave the box there until its owner returned. But what would it mean? That he, Ezeulu, was afraid of whatever power his son had imprisoned in a box. Such a story must never be told of the priest of Ulu.

He took the spear from Obika and wedged its thin end between the box and its lid. Obika tried to take the spear from him, but he would not hear it.

'Stand aside,' he told him. 'What do you think is fighting inside? Two cocks?' He clenched his teeth in an effort to lever the top open. It was not easy and the old priest was covered in sweat by the time he succeeded in forcing the box. What they saw was enough to blind a man. Ezeulu stood speechless. The women and the children who had watched from afar came running down. Ezeulu's neighbour, Anosi, who was passing by, branched in, and soon a big crowd had gathered. In the broken box lay an exhausted royal python.

'May the Great Deity forbid,' said Anosi.

'An abomination has happened,' said Akueke.

Matefi said: 'If this is medicine, may it lose its potency.'

Ezeulu let the spear fall from his hand. 'Where is Oduche?' he asked. No one answered. 'I said where is Oduche?' His voice was terrible.

Nwafo said he had gone to church. The sacred python now raised its head above the edge of the box and began to move in its dignified and unhurried way.

'Today I shall kill the boy with my own hands,' said Ezeulu as he picked up the matchet which Obika had brought at first.

'May the Great Deity forbid such a thing,' said Anosi.

'I have said it.'

Oduche's mother began to cry, and the other women joined her. Ezeulu walked slowly back to his *obi* with the matchet. The royal python slid away into the bush.

'What is the profit of crying?' Anosi asked Ugoye. 'Won't you find where your son is and tell him not to return home today?'

'He has spoken the truth, Ugoye,' said Matefi. 'Send him

away to your kinsmen. We are fortunate the python is not dead.'
From Arrow of God, by Chinua Achebe, The John Day Company, Inc., 1964.

The Geography Lesson

by Mongo Beti

Mongo Beti was born in the former French Cameroons in 1932. Rebelling against the Catholic mission where he started his schooling, he finished his education in France. He married a French girl and settled down to live and teach in Paris. There he became the centre of a lively circle, both radical and literary.

Mongo Beti's third novel, Mission to Kala, was published both in French and English (1958). His gift for dialogue is especially evident in this story of a student who returns to his native village after failing his Lycée examinations. To the student's surprise he is treated by his relatives and friends as a prodigy of learning. They defer to him as a 'scholar.'

His uncle persuades him to undertake a difficult mission to a small bush town to bring back a runaway wife, saying, '*You* are that formidable man, *you* speak with the voice of thunder, and have never suspected your own powers. Shall I tell you what your special thunder is? Your certificates, your learning, your knowledge of white men's secrets.'

When he arrives in Kala, Metza is invited to dinner with his cousin Zambo and his uncle, and finds himself the target of a barrage of questions about the world outside their personal experience.

'Are there many White children at your school?' my hostess inquired.

I said yes, there were a lot.

'More White than Coloured?'

'No; not nearly so many.'

'What are they like, these White children? Tell us what they're like,' she persisted.

'Heavens – just like children anywhere, the world over –'

'Really? Just like ordinary children?'

'Exactly,' I said. 'They have rows, and fights, and are insubordinate – there's no difference at all.'

A man's voice broke in. 'And in class,' he said, loudly. 'Are they cleverer than you in class?'

'No. They aren't either more clever or more stupid than we are. They're just the same as – us – a mixed bunch.'

'Will the learned gentleman please explain, then,' the same voice went on, in astonished tones, 'how it is that their minds work faster than ours?'

'They don't. They grasp a point no faster and no slower than we do.'

'Well, well. That's really surprising. They ought to be quicker in the uptake, though, oughtn't they?'

'Why should they?' another man's voice broke in. 'Why are you so determined that they should be quicker than our children? We don't breed young animals, do we? What are you thinking off?'

'How can you ask such a question?' the first man replied. 'It's perfectly reasonable to suppose that White children should learn faster than Black. What are they being taught? Their ancestral wisdom, not ours, isn't that so? Who invented airplanes and trains and cars and steamships? The Whites. Very well, then. Now if it was our ancestral wisdom that was taught in this school, it would be normal to expect Coloured children to learn faster than Whites, wouldn't it?'

The company were divided over this question, which provoked several fine displays of rhetoric, not least from the women. The argument went on till the man who had opposed this ingenious theory – having, to judge by the peremptory fashion in which he called the room to silence, thought up a superb and irrefutable gambit – now declared brusquely: 'Listen to me, all of you. Here's my personal opinion, for what it's worth. It's by no means certain that it was the

Whites who invented cars and airplanes and all that. When you talk about Coloured folk, you mean us, don't you? All right, we're nobodies. But what about all the other Coloured people, all over the world? How can you be sure that they don't make planes and trains and cars?'

To judge by the approving murmur which greeted it, this argument was a popular one. Finally the first man admitted that its proposer was probably right, yes, he might very well be right.

Scarcely was dinner over when my hostess began to fire a whole fusillade of questions at me. She sat next to me and went on absolutely ruthlessly, dragging detailed explanations out of me, and going back over muddled points with a needle-sharp clarity. She obviously was aware of all my weaknesses and shortcomings; she was equipped to give me the most humiliating oral I had ever been through in my life.

Then they all got down to it, and interrogated me non-stop. As there was a great number of them, they were often all asking me questions at once. This embarrassed me horribly, because I didn't know which ones to answer first: They varied in subject, but were all of equal interest. I was utterly disconcerted, and one thing embarrassed me in particular: the attitude of the women and young girls. They absolutely devoured me with their eyes, and the expressions they wore were so unequivocal that I could not help recognizing them for what they were at once, despite my natural modesty. It was like reading a young peasant girl's passionate love-letter.

Sometimes I glanced at Zambo, who squatted in a corner miserably, indifferent to the atmosphere of enthusiasm permeating the room, perhaps even hating it, but in any case the disregarded odd man out. Occasionally I caught my uncle's eye, too; he looked strangely complacent, rather like an old French peasant who has just married off his daughter to the richest, best-looking young man in the district. He was gay and pleased, and obviously willing me to make a success of the occasion.

Soon Zambo got up and left, abandoning me to my unhappy dilemma, rather as though I were a drowning man being sucked under by the current, and beyond any hope of rescue. I was the most unlucky man in the world, I thought.

Apart from anything else, I was stifling. The room was far too hot and very small; the air was thick with smoke, and smelt of palm-wine, tobacco, and chewing-gum. I made a tremendous effort, which pushed me sluggishly, like a sack of coconuts, on to the platform of benevolent resignation and cordiality reserved for scapegoats such as myself. I no longer felt any desire to discourage the attentions of my audience; I abandoned my useless and egotistic attempts at revolt. I began to chew the local gum myself, and certainly nothing I could have done would have pleased them more.

'Look at him!' they exclaimed, audibly. 'Look, he's not snobbish, for all his learning. He's chewing gum just like us.'

At such moments, conscious of all those staring eyes converging on me like so many rays, I got the feeling that the atmospheric gravity had at least doubled its pressure. There was a hurricane-lamp burning on the table, its glass bulging and rounded like an old man's belly. The light it gave out was in fact not very strong, but to me it seemed as blinding as a searchlight set up at the same distance – at point-blank range, in fact. As a result they all saw me very clearly, and I could hardly make them out at all.

I sat there wondering to what extremes of idiocy the whole business could go. Lucky for me, I thought, that my friends couldn't see me pontificating in this half-witted fashion – and, anyway, what did it matter? I realized that my affection for these people outweighed any resentment I felt at my own ridiculous position. It was certainly a serious occasion as far as they were concerned.

'And what do the Whites teach you?' my hostess was still inquiring mercilessly.

'Oh – heaps of things – '

'Come on, then: tell us them.'

'Would you understand if I did?' I snapped. The remark was greeted with a murmur of disappointment. God, what a clanger, I thought. If I'm going to stay – and I must – I've got to behave myself.

'Listen to me, my boy,' said an old man, getting to his feet and interspersing his remarks with placatory gestures, as though he were soothing a baby. 'Listen: it doesn't matter if we don't understand. Tell us all the same. For you the Whites are the real people, the people who matter, because you know their language. But we can't speak French, and we never went to school. For us you are the White man – you are the only person who can explain these mysteries to us. If you care for us at all, my son, do this thing for us. If you refuse, we've probably lost our only chance of ever being able to learn the White man's wisdom. Tell us, my son.'

He has a point there, I thought. These people were all so damnably persuasive.

'All right, then,' I said. 'They teach us – let's see – well, geography – '

'Geography?' exclaimed someone, fumbling over the unfamiliar syllables. 'What's that?'

I gave them what must have been the most feeble, certainly the most arguable definition of geography ever presented to any audience. I had never tried to formulate such a definition in my native tongue before, and now the thing had to be done for an audience who hung on my every word. Then, to make my ideas more intelligible, I decided to illustrate them with an example. I found myself (somewhat to my surprise) telling these simple people about New York – an inconceivable city to them, with its seven million inhabitants and skyscrapers of anything up to seventy-five floors, soaring up for a thousand feet. It was child's play to describe New York, probably because my only knowledge of it derived from the cinema. There was no longer any question of my drying up. I warmed to the theme, losing myself in an intoxicated sea of details. I imagined that my audience would be galvanized by the picture I conjured up; but, in fact, I went to all this trouble for nothing. The really astonishing thing, which still bothers me in retrospect, was that America left these simple-minded people stone-cold indifferent.

I quickly changed the subject, just as the other evening the young guitarist had switched his rhythms; and without exactly knowing why, I played a Russian chord, to which they at once responded. I probably acted on instinct; since I could spot at once what touched them or stirred them to enthusiasm. I must have been closer to them psychologically than I dreamed at the time.

'Russia?' they asked. 'Where's that?'

'In the east, where the sun rises,' I said. 'The inhabitants are called Russians.'

I carefully avoided mentioning the more complicated aspects of Soviet farming and spread myself as fully as possible on the kolkhoz system. A kolkhoz, I declared, with an absolutely straight face, was a kind of field held in common, where every person worked for several days a week, spending the rest of his time on his own private allotment. After the harvest, the produce from the kolkhoz was distributed to each family according to their needs. At this point in my exposition the whole room exploded like a Brock's Benefit.

'Those sound like sensible people,' said one man, and another exclaimed how fond of one another they must be. 'A very pleasant country to live in,' observed a third, and others echoed him. I was astounded at the effect I was having. Full marks for this one, boy, I thought.

I decided to work this miraculous vein till it ran out. I waxed lyrical over tractors, and State farms, and the superb administration of rural communities. I pointed out what the system had achieved – production increased tenfold since the old days of individual, private cultivation. My audience positively panted with excitement. At one point I stopped to get my breath back – I had talked myself to a standstill: lecturing is by no means a sinecure – and a youngish man took advantage of my silence to comment on my previous remarks.

'These people are very like us at bottom,' he declared. 'They've got a sense of solidarity. They stand by one another, just as we do. Look at the way our women get through their work at ploughing-time – they all spend a day in one family's fields, and the next in another's, and so on. These people, what d'you call them, boy, eh? – oh yes, Russians – well, these Russians are extraordinarily like us. If only someone would give us some tractors – one to each tribe would do – we'd do just as good work, and perhaps produce ten times the amount we do now, as well. Only one tractor per tribe! But then who on earth would ever give us a tractor?'

Another man broke in, asking me if it was true that the

men drove these tractors in the fields? He sounded a little worried. I told him yes, normally it was the men who did this type of work.

'What do the women do with their time, then?'

'They stay at home,' I said briskly. 'They stay at home to look after the children and manage the household generally. They do sometimes go out in the fields, but only to do light work. In Russia,' I added, seeing that the man was by no means resigned to this new scheme of existence, 'they consider that, since men are stronger than women, they ought to do the heavy labour; and personally I agree with them. Besides, Russian women are very pretty – they keep their looks right into middle age because they don't have to work so hard.'

I knew perfectly well that as my knowledge of real Russian life was very vague and sketchy, my only chance of coming through this ordeal unscathed was to invent my own version. The illusory nature of college learning could hardly have been better illustrated, as I learnt for myself that night. I was not without a certain pride in all I had learnt during the past academic year; yet at the first real test of my knowledge – a test imposed by genuine circumstance, not under the artificial conditions of an examination-room – I had already discovered vast gaps in the frontiers of my tiny kingdom. Now I was desperately trying to plug these gaps, and straining my imagination to the uttermost in the process.

Everything finally has to come to an end, and at last the party broke up. My hostess thanked me for the evening's entertainment, and her husband promised to deliver a little present for me the following morning at my uncle's home.

As we walked back by ourselves my uncle said: 'They'll talk about you here for ages, boy.'

From Mission to Kala, by Mongo Beti, Heinemann Educational Books Ltd., 1958.

My Husband's Tongue Is Bitter

by Okot p'Bitek

Okot p'Bitek is a young philosopher and poet who was born in 1931 of the Acholi tribe in Northern Uganda. Educated both in Africa and England, he has studied education, law, and anthropology. Football and the theatre are among his other interests. He has had one novel published in the Luo language and two long poems in English, *Song of Lawino* (1966) and *Song of Ocol* (1970). He served as Director of the National Cultural Centre in Uganda and founded the Gulu Festival.

The selection which follows is from *Song of Lawino*. It is a wife's lament which can be heard all over Africa. She voices the sorrows of a woman brought up in traditional tribal society who is married to a man educated in the ways of the white man.

My clansmen, I cry
Listen to my voice:
The insults of my man
Are painful beyond bearing.

My husband abuses me together with my parents;
He says terrible things about my mother
And I am so ashamed!

He abuses me in English
And he is so arrogant.

My husband pours scorn
On Black People,
He behaves like a hen
That eats its own eggs
A hen that should be imprisoned
Under a basket.

His eyes grow large
Deep black eyes
Ocol's eyes resemble those of the Nile Perch!
He becomes fierce
Like a lioness with cubs,
He begins to behave like a mad hyena.

He says Black People are primitive
And their ways are utterly harmful,
Their dances are mortal sins
They are ignorant, poor and diseased!

Ocol says he is a modern man,
A progressive and civilized man.
He says he has read extensively and widely
And he can no longer live with a thing like me
Who cannot distinguish between good and bad,
He says I am just a village woman,
I am of the old type,
And no longer attractive.

Ocol is no longer in love with the old type.
He is in love with a modern girl;
The name of the beautiful one
Is Clementine.

Brother, when you see Clementine!
The beautiful one aspires
To look like a white woman;
Her lips are red-hot
Like glowing charcoal,
She resembles the wild cat
That has dipped its mouth in blood,
Her mouth is like raw yaws
It looks like an open ulcer,
Like the mouth of a fiend!
Tina dusts powder on her face
And it looks so pale;
She resembles the wizard
Getting ready for the midnight dance;

And she believes
That this is beautiful
Because it resembles the face of a white woman!
Her body resembles
The ugly coat of the hyena;
Her neck and arms
Have real human skins!
She looks as if she has been struck
By lightning;
Or burnt like the *kongoni*
In a fire hunt.

I am not unfair to my husband,
I do not complain
Because he wants another woman
Whether she is young or aged!
Who has ever prevented men
From wanting women?

The competition for a man's love
Is fought at the cooking place
When he returns from the field
Or from the hunt.

You win him with a hot bath
and sour porridge.
The wife who brings her meal first
Whose food is good to eat,
Whose dish is hot
Whose face is bright
And whose heart is clean
And whose eyes are not dark
Like the shadows:

The wife who jokes freely
Who eats in the open
Not in the bed room,
One who is not dull
Like stale beer,

Such is the woman who becomes
The head-dress keeper.

I do not block my husband's path
From his new wife.
If he likes, let him build for her
An iron roofed house on the hill!
I do not complain,
My grass thatched house is enough for me.

I am not angry
With the woman with whom
I share my husband,
I do not fear to compete with her.

Listen Ocol, my old friend,
The ways of your ancestors
Are good,
Their customs are solid
And not hollow
They are not thin, not easily breakable
They cannot be blown away.
By the winds
Because their roots reach deep into the soil.

I do not understand
The way of foreigners
But I do not despise their customs.
Why should you despise yours?
Listen, my husband,
You are the son of a Chief.
The pumpkin in the old homestead
Must not be uprooted!

From Song of Lawino, by Okot p'Bitek, East African Publishing House, 1966.

The Untilled Field

by Joseph Waiguru

Joseph Waiguru was born in Nyeri, Kenya, in 1939. He was a student at Makerere University College, Kampala, from 1959 to 1964, during the first years of Independence. He studied English, Economics, and Political Science. His work in English under David Cook encouraged him to combine criticism with creative writing. His stories and poems have been broadcast by the British Broadcasting Company African Service and by Radio Uganda, and are now published for the first time in David Cook's anthology, *Origin East Africa*.

Mwangi thought of nobody else but his wife Wanjiku. She was lazy; always going to work late in the day when everybody else had already done half their digging. By the time she reached the field, it was already so hot that to lift a hoe was almost a torture. The heat of the sun disturbed the flies from their rest so that they buzzed around her as she slowly lifted her tool. She had to drop it again to strike the biting fly. There was no point in continuing to labour. After all she would come here tomorrow and the day after. Even the day after that she would be here.

She sat down in the cool shade of a *muthaithi* tree and soon fell asleep. Mwangi watched her from afar, where he was herding his cattle. By now it was his field alone which lay untilled, and the rains were near. An hour went by, two hours, three hours and Wanjiku still slept. Was she dead? Could a snake have bitten her? He would have heard cries. Mwangi decided to find out.

He left his cattle and slowly approached the spot where his wife lay. He looked back to see whether the cattle would stray far before he returned to them. Satisfied that they would not, he moved on. He quickened his step, hoping that she would wake up before he reached her. He did not want to show her that he had all along been watching her. But he would never be satisfied until he knew whether or not his wife's expression betrayed any guilty conscience for the neglect of her duties. He changed his pace. Quietly he stalked her as a lion stealthily hunts a deer, or like a cobra just about to strike. He feared to make a rustle.

Mwangi remembered the cows and goats he had paid her father as a dowry. The marriage feast surpassed any he had ever seen, or even heard of. Is this the wife he had married, the woman he had so dearly paid for? Was she created only for child-bearing? What was she for? He would soon learn from the appearance of her face when asleep. He reached her.

There she was, sleeping like a log, except that a log does not breathe. The sight shocked him. Where he had expected to find at least a slight element of guilt, he found only a pure, peaceful, calm face – only blissful happiness. Wanjiku was content to lie idle, a basket, a hoe and a *panga* by her side.

He stood there, not knowing what to do next. His mind was as blank as a white sheet. At last, his lips set as if to smile and then changed into a grin which looked sinister. His jaw dropped, showing milky-white teeth. He thought of beating her with the thick walking-stick he was carrying and then that evening sending her packing to her father's. No, he would gain nothing by such an action.

After all, women were just little, defenceless creatures. He was annoyed when he realized he could not beat her. Oh, but she was beautiful too; He knelt down and touched her lips with the back of his right hand, moving the fingers along them. She stirred and turned face downwards, but did not open her eyes. Mwangi was furious with himself and with her. He turned to see what work she had done – there was no sign of freshly dug ground. She should have finished this field since she informed him that she had started on it, but at this rate she would not have completed even half of it before the rains poured madly down. Would she ever wake? After deciding not to disturb her, he quickly went back to his cattle.

Mwangi thought for a moment. Then he rounded up his animals and drove them home at the greatest speed the beasts could manage. He shut them in a shed, though it was only two o'clock, and hurriedly took a hoe from his hut. There was no time to lose, and within fifteen minutes he was back in the field. Wanjiku was still sleeping. He would not wake her up: that he had resolved the moment he decided to take his cattle home.

Mwangi planted his feet firmly on the ground and lifted the hoe high over his head. He struck another and yet another. Thud, thud, thud went the hoe, on and on. He laboured and was never tired. Drops of sweat flowed down his face and their sour taste only added more energy to his stout arms.

Lumps of earth were following him as he proceeded farther and farther away from where he started. He neither looked back nor forwards lest the length of the field he had to dig should discourage him. All he saw was the place where he had to push in his hoe. He laboured on.

He was twenty yards when Wanjiku woke up and saw him. What was it? She looked up at the sun in the sky and knew it was half past three; the time she started collecting firewood. Was she always sleeping like this? She watched mesmerized as he dug and dug.

Mwangi stopped for breath without looking back. The sweat was too much. His shirt and trousers were glued to his body. He dropped the hoe, took off his clothes and then cut a banana leaf which he tied round his waist. He then picked up the hoe, lifted it and once again resumed his work.

As Wanjiku watched, he moved farther and farther away from her. He furiously attacked the ground which was becoming as stubborn as a mule. His black frame dripped wet and as drops of sweat flowed down his whole body, they cut lines in the red dust which had stuck to his skin. The more he turned the ground, the madder he grew.

Suddenly, Wanjiku stood up and picked up her hoe. She rushed to his side and wanted to stop him. He barked at her and she gave up. Within a few minutes, he was ahead of her by six feet. He would not rest until the work was over. Was he her husband any more? Certainly.

With a force she had never felt before, she went to his

right-hand side and started digging. She would dig as long as he dug, and stop when he stopped. If they were to die, they would die together. She soon caught up and fell into step with him. The earth was softer than she had ever known it to be. They dug and never stopped to see what work they had done.

Neither was thinking of the other but only of their field. The sun was, however, faster than they were and the last flickers of light would soon disappear. They went on and on, and neither dared to speak.

It was cool now, and a soft breeze blew over them but was not enough to dry away the sweat. In unison, they attacked the enemy who had brought them together. It grew dark but they never thought of going home. They saw the edge of the field and stopped petrified. Only two feet away! They looked at one another and then at the edge. They turned back and could not see where they had started. With smiles they embraced and fell down. There they lay till the following morning when they woke up as if from a dream, completely satisfied of their future life together.

THREE SOUSSOU TALES

The Sweetest Thing

There is in this world something
That surpasses all other things
in sweetness
It is sweeter than honey
It is sweeter than salt
It is sweeter than sugar
It is sweeter than all
existing things.
This thing is sleep.
When you are conquered by sleep
Nothing can ever prevent you
Nothing can stop you from sleeping.
When you are conquered by sleep
And numerous millions arrive
  Millions arrive to disturb you
  But millions will find you asleep.

The Moon

The moon lights the earth
It lights the earth but still
The night must remain the night.
The night cannot be like the day.
The moon cannot dry our washing
Just like a woman cannot be a man
Just like a black can never be white

The Well

There is a well
That has five kinds of water.
There is sugared water
and salty water
There is tasteless water
And bitter water.
The fifth water is red
red like blood.
This well is the head.

The Winner

by Barbara Kimenye

Barbara Kimenye is a Ugandan journalist, author of two collections of short stories, *Kalasanda* and *Kalasanda Revisited* both published in 1965. In these stories, she recreates the ups and downs of everyday life in rural Uganda. The time is now. Modern inventions such as automobiles, radios, and telegrams exist side by side with the traditional way of life.

The people in *The Winner* live in mud and wattle huts behind which each householder owns a small bit of land, his *shamba*. Here he grows most of his own food – bananas and coffee, sweet potatoes, beans, and cabbages – with perhaps a small surplus to give away or sell. The old men have their cronies and the women their ambitions and their jealousies.

When Pius Ndawula won the football pools, overnight he seemed to become the most popular man in Buganda. Hosts of relatives converged upon him from the four corners of the kingdom; cousins and nephews, nieces and uncles, of whose existence he had never before been aware, turned up in Kalasanda by the busload, together with crowds of individuals who, despite their downtrodden appearance, assured Pius that they and they alone were capable of seeing that his money was properly invested – preferably in their own particular businesses!

Also lurking around Pius's unpretentious mud hut were newspaper reporters, slick young men weighed down with cameras and sporting loud checked caps or trilbies set at conspicuously jaunty angles, and serious young men from Radio Uganda who were anxious to record Pius's delight at his astonishing luck for the edification of the Uganda listening public.

The rest of Kalasanda were so taken by surprise that they could only call and briefly congratulate Pius before being elbowed out of the way by his more garrulous relations. All, that is to say, except Pius's greatest friend Salongo, the custodian of the Ssabalangira's tomb. He came and planted himself firmly in the house, and nobody attempted to move him. Almost blind, and very lame, he tottered out with the aid of a stout stick. Just to see him arrive had caused a minor sensation in the village, for he hadn't left the tomb for years. But recognizing at last a chance to house Ssabalangira's remains in a state befitting his former glory, made the slow tortuous journey worthwhile to Salongo.

Nantondo hung about long enough to have her picture taken with Pius. Or rather, she managed to slip beside him just as the cameras clicked and so it was that every Uganda newspaper, on the following day, carried a front-page photograph of 'Mr Pius Ndawula and his happy wife,' a caption that caused Pius to shake with rage and threaten legal proceedings, but over which Nantondo gloated as she proudly showed it to everybody who visited.

'Tell us, Mr Ndawula, what do you intend to do with all the money you have won . . .?'

'Tell us, Mr Ndawula, how often have you completed pools coupons . . .?'

'Tell us . . . Tell us . . . Tell us . . .'

Pius's head was reeling under this bombardment of questions, and he was even more confused by Salongo's constant nudging and muttered advice to 'Say nothing!' Nor did the relatives make things easier. Their persistent clamouring for his attention, and the way they kept shoving their children under his nose, made it impossible for him to think, let alone talk.

It isn't at all easy, when you have lived for sixty-five years in complete obscurity, to adjust yourself in a matter of hours to the role of a celebrity, and the strain was beginning to tell.

Behind the hut – Pius had no proper kitchen – gallons of tea were being boiled, whilst several of the female cousins were employed in ruthlessly hacking down the bunches of *matoke* from his meagre plantains, to cook food for everybody. One woman – she had introduced herself as Cousin Sarah – discovered Pius's hidden store of banana beer, and dished it out to all and sundry as though it were her own. Pius had become very wary of Cousin Sarah. He didn't like the way in which she kept loudly remarking that he needed a woman about the place, and he was even more seriously alarmed when suddenly Salongo gave him a painful dig in the ribs and muttered, 'You'll have to watch that one – she's a sticker!'

Everybody who came wanted to see the telegram that

The Winner

announced Pius's win. When it had arrived at the Ggombolola Headquarters – the postal address of everyone living within a radius of fifteen miles – Musisi had brought it out personally, delighted to be the bearer of such good tidings. At Pius's request he had gone straight away to tell Salongo, and then back to his office to send an acknowledgment on behalf of Pius to the pools firm, leaving the old man to dream rosy dreams.

An extension of his small coffee *shamba*, a new roof on his house – or maybe an entirely new house – concrete blocks this time, with a verandah perhaps. Then there were hens. Salongo and he had always said there was money in hens these days, now that the women ate eggs and chicken; not that either of them agreed with the practice. Say what you liked, women who ate chicken and eggs were fairly asking to be infertile! That woman Welfare officer who came around snooping occasionally, tried to say it was all nonsense, that chicken meat and eggs made bigger and better babies. Well, they might look bigger and better, but nobody could deny that they were fewer! Which only goes to show.

But news spreads fast in Africa – perhaps the newspapers have contacts in the pools offices. Anyway, before the telegram had even reached Pius, announcements were appearing in the local newspapers, and Pius was still quietly lost in his private dreams when the first batch of visitors arrived. At first, he was at a loss to understand what was happening. People he hadn't seen for years and only recognized with difficulty fell upon him with cries of joy.

'Cousin Pius, the family are delighted!'

'Cousin Pius, why have you not visited us all this time?'

Pius was pleased to see his nearest and dearest gathered around him. It warmed his old heart once more to find himself in the bosom of his family, and he welcomed them effusively. The second crowd to arrive were no less well received, but there was a marked coolness on the part of their forerunners.

However, as time had gone by and the flood of strange faces had gained momentum, Pius's *shamba* had come to resemble a political meeting. All to be seen from the door of the house was a turbulent sea of white *kanzus* and brilliant *busutis*, and the house itself was full of people and tobacco smoke.

The precious telegram was passed from hand to hand until it was reduced to a limp fragment of paper with the lettering partly obliterated: not that it mattered very much, for only a few members of the company could read English.

'Now, Mr Ndawula, we are ready to take the recording.' The speaker was a slight young man wearing a checked shirt. 'I shall ask you a few questions, and you simply answer me in your normal voice.' Pius looked at the leather box with its two revolving spools, and licked his lips.

'Say nothing!' came a hoarse whisper from Salongo.

The young man steadfastly ignored him, and went ahead in his best BBC manner. 'Well, first of all, Mr Ndawula, let me congratulate you on your winning the pools. Would you like to tell our listeners what it feels like suddenly to find yourself rich?' There was an uncomfortable pause, during which Pius stared mesmerized at the racing spools and the young man tried frantically to span the gap by asking, 'I mean, have you any plans for the future?'

Pius swallowed audibly, and opened his mouth to say something, but shut it again when Salongo growled, 'Tell him nothing!'

The young man snapped off the machine, shaking his head in exasperation. 'Look here, sir, all I want you to do is to say something – I'm not asking you to make a speech. Now, I'll tell you what. I shall ask you again what it feels like suddenly to come into money, and you say something like "It was a wonderful surprise, and naturally I feel very pleased" – and will you ask your friend not to interrupt! Got it? Okay, off we go!'

The machine was again switched on, and the man brightly put the question, 'Now, Mr Ndawula, what does it feel like to win the pools?'

Pius swallowed, then quickly chanted in a voice all off key, 'It was a wonderful surprise and naturally I feel very happy and will you ask your friend not to interrupt!' The young man nearly wept. This happened to be his first assignment as a radio interviewer, and it looked like being his last. He switched off the machine and mourned his lustreless future, groaning.

At that moment Cousin Sarah caught his eye. 'Perhaps I can help you,' she said. 'I am Mr Ndawula's cousin.' She made this pronouncement in a manner that suggested Pius had no others. The young man brightened considerably. 'Well, madam, if you could tell me something about Mr Ndawula's plans, I would be most grateful.'

Cousin Sarah folded her arms across her imposing bosom, and when the machine again started up, she was off. Yes, Mr Ndawula was very happy about the money. No, she didn't think he had any definite plans on how to spend it – with all these people about he didn't have time to think. Yes, Mr Ndawula lived completely alone, but she was prepared to stay and look after him for as long as he needed her. Here a significant glance passed between the other women in the room, who clicked their teeth and let out long 'Eeeeeeehs!' of incredulity. Yes, she believed she was Mr Ndawula's nearest living relative by marriage . . .

Pius listened to her confident aplomb with growing horror, whilst Salongo frantically nudged him and whispered, 'There! What did I tell you? That woman's a sticker.'

Around three in the afternoon, *matoke* and tea were served – the *matoke* on wide fresh plaintain leaves, since Pius owned only three plates, and the tea in anything handy – tin cans, old jars, etc. – because he was short of cups, too.

Pius ate very little, but he was glad of the tea. He had shaken hands with so many people that his arms ached, and he was tired of the chatter and the comings and goings in his house of all these strangers. Most of all he was tired of Cousin Sarah, who insisted on treating him like an idiot invalid. She kept everybody else at bay, as far as she possibly could, and when one woman plonked a sticky fat baby on his lap, Cousin Sarah dragged the child away as though it were infectious. Naturally, a few cross words were exchanged between Sarah and the fond mother, but by this time Pius was past caring.

Yosefu Mukasa and Kibuka called in the early evening, when some of the relatives were departing with effusive promises to come again tomorrow. They were both alarmed at the weariness they saw on Pius's face. The old man looked utterly worn out, his skin grey and sickly. Also, they were a bit taken aback by the presence of Cousin Sarah, who pressed them to take tea and behaved in every respect as though she was mistress of the house.

'I believe my late husband knew you very well, sir,' she told Yosefu. 'He used to be a Miruka chief in Buyaga County. His name was Kivumbi.'

'Ah, yes,' Yosefu replied. 'I remember Kivumbi very well indeed. We often hunted together. I was sorry to hear of his death. He was a good man.'

Cousin Sarah shrugged her shoulders. 'Yes, he was a good man. But what the Lord giveth, He also taketh away.' Thus was the late Kivumbi dismissed from the conversation.

Hearing all this enabled Pius to define the exact relationship between himself and Cousin Sarah, and even by Kiganda standards it was virtually nonexistent, for the late Kivumbi had been the stepson of one of Pius's cousins.

'Your stroke of luck seems to have exhausted you, Pius,' Kibuka remarked, when he and Yosefu were seated on the rough wooden chairs brought forth by Cousin Sarah.

Salongo glared at the world in general and snarled, 'Of course he is exhausted. Who wouldn't be with all these scavengers collected to pick his bones?' Pius hushed him as one would a child. 'No, no, Salongo. It is quite natural that my family should gather round me at a time like this. Only I fear I am perhaps a little too old for all this excitement.'

Salongo spat expertly through the open doorway, narrowly missing a group of guests who were preparing to bed down, and said, 'That woman doesn't think he is too old. She's out to catch him. I've seen her type elsewhere.'

Yosefu's mouth quirked with amusement at the thought that 'elsewhere' could only mean the Ssabalangira's tomb, which Salongo had guarded for the better part of his adult life. 'Well, she's a fine woman,' he remarked. 'But see here, Pius,' he went on, 'don't be offended by my proposal, but wouldn't it be better if you came and stayed with us at Mutunda for tonight? Miriamu would love to have you, and you look as though you need a good night's rest, which you wouldn't get here – those relatives of yours outside are preparing a fire and are ready to dance the night away!'

'I think that's a wonderful idea!' said Cousin Sarah, bouncing in to remove the tea cups. 'You go with Mr Mukasa, Cousin Pius. The change will do you as much good as the rest. And don't worry about your home – I shall stay here and look after things.'

Pius hesitated. 'Well, I think I shall be all right here – I don't like to give Miriamu any extra work . . .'

Salongo muttered, 'Go to Yosefu's. You don't want to be left alone in the house with that woman – there's no knowing what she might get up to . . .'

'I'll pack a few things for you, Pius,' announced Cousin Sarah and bustled off before anything more could be said, pausing only long enough to give Salongo a look that was meant to wither him on the spot.

So Pius found himself being driven away to Mutunda in Yosefu's car, enjoying the pleasant sensation of not having to bother about a thing. Salongo too had been given a lift to as near the tomb as the car could travel, and his wizened old face was contorted into an irregular smile, for Pius had promised to help him build a new house for the Ssabalangira. For him the day had been well spent, despite Cousin Sarah.

Pius spent an enjoyable evening with the Mukasas. They had a well-cooked supper, followed by a glass of cool beer as they sat back and listened to the local news on the radio. Pius had so far relaxed as to tell the Mukasas modestly that he had been interviewed by Radio Uganda that morning, and when Radio Newsreel was announced they waited breathlessly to hear his voice. But instead of Pius, Cousin Sarah came booming over the air. Until that moment, the old man had completely forgotten the incident of the tape-recording. In fact, he had almost forgotten Cousin Sarah. Now it all came back to him with a shiver of apprehension. Salongo was right. That woman did mean business! It was a chilling thought. However, it didn't cause him to lose any sleep. He slept like a cherub, as if he didn't have a care in the world.

Because he looked so refreshed in the morning, Miriamu insisted on keeping him at Mutunda for another day. 'I know you feel better, but after seeing you yesterday, I think a little holiday with us will do you good. Go home tomorrow, when the excitement has died down a bit,' she advised.

Soon after lunch, as Pius was taking a nap in a chair on the verandah, Musisi drove up in the Land-Rover, with Cousin Sarah by his side. Miriamu came out to greet them, barely disguising her curiosity about the formidable woman about whom she had heard so much. The two women sized each other up and decided to be friends.

Meanwhile, Musisi approached the old man. 'Sit down, son,' Pius waved him to a chair at his side. 'Miriamu feeds me so well it's all I can do to keep awake.'

'I am glad you are having a rest, sir.' Musisi fumbled in the pocket of his jacket. 'There is another telegram for you. Shall I read it?' The old man sat up expectantly and said, 'If you'll be so kind.'

Musisi first read the telegram in silence, then he looked at Pius and commented, 'Well, sir, I'm afraid it isn't good news.'

'Not good news? Has somebody died?'

Musisi smiled. 'Well, no. It isn't really as bad as that. The thing is, the pools firm say that owing to an unfortunate oversight they omitted to add, in the first telegram, that the prize money is to be shared among three hundred other people.'

Pius was stunned. Eventually he murmured, 'Tell me, how much does that mean I shall get?'

'Three hundred into seventeen thousand pounds won't give you much over a thousand shillings.'

To Musisi's astonishment, Pius sat back and chuckled. 'More than a thousand shillings!' he said. 'Why that's a lot of money!'

'But it's not, when you expected so much more.'

'I agree. And yet, son, what would I have done with all those thousands of pounds? I am getting past the age when I need a lot.'

Miriamu brought a mat on to the verandah and she and Cousin Sarah made themselves comfortable near the men. 'What a disappointment!' cried Miriamu, but Cousin Sarah sniffed and said, 'I agree with Cousin Pius. He wouldn't know what to do with seventeen thousand pounds, and the family would be hanging round his neck for evermore.'

At mention of Pius's family, Musisi frowned. 'I should

warn you, sir, those relatives of yours have made a terrific mess of your *shamba* – your plantains have been stripped – and Mrs Kivumbi here,' nodding at Sarah, 'was only just in time to prevent them digging up your sweet potatoes.'

'Yes, Cousin Pius,' added Sarah. 'It will take us some time to put the *shamba* back in order. They've trodden down a whole bed of young beans.'

'Oh, dear,' said Pius weakly. 'This is dreadful news.'

'Don't worry. They will soon disappear when I tell them there is no money, and then I shall send for a couple of my grandsons to come and help us do some replanting.' Pius could not help but admire the way Sarah took things in her stride.

Musisi rose from his chair. 'I'm afraid I can't stay any longer, so I will go now and help Cousin Sarah clear the crowd, and see you tomorrow to take you home.' He and Sarah climbed back into the Land-Rover and Sarah waved energetically until the vehicle was out of sight.

'Your cousin is a fine woman,' Miriamu told Pius, before going indoors. Pius merely grunted, but for some odd reason he felt the remark to be a compliment to himself.

All was quiet at Pius's home when Musisi brought him home next day. He saw at once that his *shamba* was wellnigh wrecked, but his drooping spirits quickly revived when Sarah placed a mug of steaming tea before him, and sat on a mat at his feet, explaining optimistically how matters could be remedied. Bit by bit he began telling her what he planned to do with the prize money, ending with, 'Of course, I shan't be able to do everything now, especially since I promised Salongo something for the tomb.'

Sarah poured some more tea and said, 'Well, I think the roof should have priority. I noticed last night that there are several leaks. And whilst we're about it, it would be a good idea to build another room on and a small outside kitchen. Mud and wattle is cheap enough, and then the whole place can be plastered. You can still go ahead and extend your coffee. And as for hens, well, I have six good layers at home, as well as a fine cockerel. I'll bring them over!'

Pius looked at her in silence for a long time. She is a finelooking woman, he thought, and that blue *busuti* suits her.

Nobody would ever take her for a grandmother – but why is she so anxious to throw herself at me?

'You sound as if you are planning to come and live here,' he said at last, trying hard to sound casual.

Sarah turned to face him and replied, 'Cousin Pius, I shall be very frank with you. Six months ago my youngest son got married and brought his wife to live with me. She's a very nice girl, but somehow I can't get used to having another woman in the house. My other son is in Kampala, and although I know I would be welcome there, he too has a wife, and three children, so if I went there I wouldn't be any better off.

'When I saw that bit about you in the paper, I suddenly remembered – although I don't expect you to – how you were at my wedding and so helpful to everybody. Well, I thought to myself, here is somebody who needs a good housekeeper, who needs somebody to keep the leeches off, now that he has come into money. I came along right away to take a look at you, and I can see I did the right thing. You do need me.' She hesitated for a moment, and then said, 'Only you might prefer to stay alone. . . . I'm so used to having my own way, I never thought about that before.'

Pius cleared his throat. 'You're a very impetuous woman,' was all he could find to say.

A week later, Pius wandered over to the tomb and found Salongo busily polishing the Ssabalangira's weapons. 'I thought you were dead,' growled the custodian, 'it is so long since you came here – but then this tomb thrives on neglect. Nobody cares that one of Buganda's greatest men lies here.'

'I have been rather busy,' murmured Pius. 'But I didn't forget my promise to you. Here! I've brought you a hundred shillings, and I only wish it could have been more. At least it will buy a few cement blocks.'

Salongo took the money and looked at it as if it were crawling with lice. Grudgingly he thanked Pius and then remarked, 'Of course, you will find life more expensive now that you are keeping a woman in the house.'

'I suppose Nantondo told you,' Pius smiled sheepishly.

'Does it matter who told me?' the custodian replied. 'Anyway, never say I didn't warn you. Next thing she'll want will be ring marriage!'

Pius gave an uncertain laugh. 'As a matter of fact, one of the reasons I came up here was to invite you to the wedding — it's next month.'

Salongo carefully laid down the spear he was rubbing upon a piece of clean barkcloth and stared at his friend as if he had suddenly grown another head. 'What a fool you are! And all this stems from your scribbling noughts and crosses on a bit of squared paper. I knew it would bring no good! At your age you ought to have more sense. Well, all I can advise is that you run while you still have a chance.'

For a moment Pius was full of misgivings. Was he, after all, behaving like a fool? Then he thought of Sarah, and the wonders she had worked with his house and his *shamba* in the short time they had been together. He felt reassured.

'Well, I'm getting married, and I expect to see you at both the church and the reception, and if you don't appear, I shall want to know the reason why!' He was secretly delighted at the note of authority in his voice, and Salongo's face was the picture of astonishment.

'All right,' he mumbled, 'I shall try and come. Before you go, cut a bunch of bananas to take back to your good lady, and there might be some cabbage ready at the back. I suppose I've got to hand it to her. She's the real winner!'

The Epic of Liyongo

by Muhammed Kijuma

Muhammed Kijuma is a twentieth-century Swahili poet who has written in traditional verse about the Swahili hero, Liyongo. *The Epic of Liyongo*, one of the most famous Swahili legends, is often compared to the King Arthur cycle in English. Both are a mixture of myth and history. The theme of the Liyongo epic is a family feud, a struggle between Liyongo and his cousin for the sultanate of Shaka, or Shagga, in the thirteenth century.

The word *Swahili*, which literally means 'coast people' in Arabic, describes the people of Kenya, Tanzania, and Zanzibar, who are descendants of native Bantu tribes and Arab traders. Their language is a mixture of Bantu and Arabic that has evolved over a long period. Swahili is the *lingua franca* of East Africa and is also used in Tanzania as the official language of the National Assembly. It is spoken by more people than any other indigenous language.

Swahili poetry exists in its own right as an important cultural heritage. Originally, it was used to teach the spirit and practice of the Islamic religion. There are many Swahili proverbs, homilies, praise-songs, love songs, serenades, and legends which have been preserved orally for hundreds of years. Among all these *The Epic of Liyongo* is a favourite, a sad and tragic story which brings tears to the eyes of its listeners, no matter how many times they hear it.

As Liyongo grew in perfection   he became a mature man   he was a true man   and his beauty of appearance increased.
He was of glorious stature   very broad and tall   he became famous in the provinces   and people came to behold him.
If he should stare at you   you would faint right off   death would be near   because of the fear that has entered into you.

Rumours came   to the Sultan a thousand of them   and he determined with guile   to kill him (Liyongo), understand.
And the Sultan, let me say   feared this man   that he would rob him of his kingdom   and he thought of him with suspicion.
Liyongo understood   that they looked for a way to kill him and so he withdrew himself from Pate   and journeyed on the mainland.
And when the Sultain perceived   that he (Liyongo) had fled to the forest   he made contact with the Sanye tribesmen   and with Dahalo as well . . .

The Epic of Liyongo

One day they said   Now let us eat like gentlefolk   the *kikoa* feast is very delicious   a feast that does not fail.

And for the *kikoa* let us eat the dum-palm fruit   we will not come to the end of being satisfied with it   those who eat the dum-palm fruit   one man shall climb each day.

When their plan was finished   they went their way   for those who get the fruit   one man climbs up (alone).

And their idea was   that on the day when he (Liyongo) would climb up   they would all shoot him   with one swift volley.

They all made their contribution   and only Liyongo remained   it is you now, they told him   we want (the fruit), understand.

Liyongo spoke quickly   Choose a dum-palm   the fruits that you like   so that I may pluck them down for you.

Walking in single file   to choose a tall tree   until they saw it   they said to him, It is this one.

When Liyongo saw it   (that) it was a very tall tree   he understood the meaning   of those (things) that he had thought about them.

For he was always cautious   (even) while he slept he was on guard   he knew that they purposed evil   all of them together.

And he said to them, Wait   and he took from a shaft arrows and put (one) in the bow-string   and brought down the fruit for them.

He brought down the ripe topmost cluster   a cluster with many fruits   and they were all agape   and a wonder filled their hearts.

And they murmured in their hearts   Who can get the better of him?   This man is undefeatable   and (to try to best him) is to want to be destroyed . . .

Liyongo, what I tell you now   was Shaha of the *gungu* tourneys and of the *mwao* dance   he was their leader   he excelled them all.

The Sultan explained   to the leaders of the town   and said to them in private   Proclaim a *gungu* tourney, he told them.

(A dance) for men and women   and invite Liyongo   I intend to seize him   and this is a secret that I have told you.

And if he gets wind of this   and he Liyongo runs away (if you have told him of this   I will slay you all.

And this Sultan   (if he sought) to slay, (no man) could gainsay him   for when he spake it was with certainty   he would fulfil his word at once.

The leaders sent out the invitation   to Liyongo they proclaimed   we will prepare a *mwao* dance   so that we may all be together.

And they prepared the *mwao* dance   with every customary due   the Sultan sent   his men-at-arms about a hundred in number.

They marched in column   with spears and bows and battle-staves   and they seized Liyongo   and he was put in jail.

He was put in jail   and was shut up in a cell   with soldiers at the door   taking turn to watch.

Then there was debate   whether he should be killed (they said) Let us keep away from this evil of his   I am afraid of Liyongo.

The Sultan thought   It is better to kill him   for if he is spared there would be danger   for he would embroil me in some scheme.

Let him deprive me of my kingdom   and I would gnaw the finger of repentance   it is better for me that this fellow   be killed at once.

His kinsmen then he called   to plan with them the slaying   and they agreed, Indeed, that is the thing to do   we are of the same opinion.

They sent a slave-messenger   to Liyongo and said   Death is certain   they have sent me to tell you.

What is there that you wish?   The Sultan has sent me   you will receive it most certainly   so that you may make your farewells to the world.

He has told you, our Lord   and he has sent me as messenger   that in the space of three days   understand you will be killed.

And he replied, Do not be sure   tell the Sultan   that

The Epic of Liyongo

I wish for a *mwao* dance   and for a *gungu* tourney as well.
And when the Sultan's messenger   had left the cell there entered a servant-maid   and she brought him food.
And when his (Liyongo's) mother for certain   sent good food   the soldiers would deprive him of it   and would eat the food.
Whenever they brought food to him   the soldiers confiscated it   but on this day he said (to the slave-girl)   Greet my mother for me.
And he spoke (in secret) rhyme   Go and tell her   let my mother prepare   these things that I have told you of (i.e. in the following poem).

O maiden, I send you, for you have not yet been sent,
Tell my mother, who is innocent and guileless.
Let her make a loaf for me and put inside a file   So that I can cut through these handcuffs and break my chains.
Let me cross these walls and the roof shall be broken through. Let me kill men and as they fight I will laugh.
Let me go into the reeds and creep like a fierce snake.
Let me enter the forest and roar like a fierce lion.
I am like a lone tree alone in the treeless wilderness
Without kinsfolk or friends, alone I am left an orphan.
Only my mother is left, to whose whelp's cry her answering will be lent.

Saada perceived his plan   and his mother set the fires   to make a loaf of bran   and sent him the bread.
This bread, understand was of about eight pounds weight   and she placed the file inside   and Liyongo received her (the slave-girl).
When the soldiers saw   that it was made of bran they cursed   Only slaves eat loaves of bran   take it to him, go on, get in.
But Liyongo in his cell   broke the loaf in secret   and he saw the file inside   and was filled with joy.
And when night was come   and they made ready for the

dances   and according to custom prepared   the gongs, horns, and trumpets.

With the drums and much hand-clapping   and no one being absent   it was just like a wedding   and the people watched.

They spread out (rugs) of thread of gold   with silken (fabrics) of great beauty   and they sang poems midst handclaps and drumming.

And the poems are these   which they sang together   the people sang the chorus   and Liyongo sang the air.

'Mringwari, drummers and chorus, come, you are called by the Lord Liyongo   come, Lord Liyongo calls you and his kinsman Shaha Mwengo.

Sit on the ceremonial divan, let them gather the dancers of the pirouette   let them gather the graceful dancers skilled in composing enigmas.

Who know how to rhyme and to dance with the straining of the neck you are called, hurry, arise and go, you nobles of high place.

There is a *gungu* ceremony, a nuptial dance, Liyongo's sister is being wed   what time people cannot pause in the hall because of the crowd.

And when you go don your fine robes and sprinkle yourselves with perfume   perfume yourselves with choice *tibu*, fine-ground with admixtures of perfuming powders.

And with incense of ambergris and of aloe-wood, cense your spotless garments   cense your silken garments and cloths for your loins free from all blemish.

Take the young girls with great show and receive the young men with united chorus   and the hand-clappers and singers, take the young girls in groups.

Haste, haste, rise up, you are called, today the door is wide   there are baskets and baskets of presents and gifts by the hundred.

Of silver and Indian crystal and chains for adorning the neck   and baskets and baskets of garments in the great hall of the Lord Liyongo.

No sooner the people arrive in the hall than there is a great throng   with the tall folk on tip-toe and the short

ones straining their necks.
And everyone says, This is joyful; both those who walk upright and those who are bent   for gaining the best of the matter without surfeit of strolling about.
At that moment Liyongo arose and calmed his heart and suppressed his rage   and he calmed himself as he sang while the maidens and youths danced around.
And those people cried out all together, It is Liyongo the poet, of that there is no mistake   it is the poet chieftain, the poet who came to the coastland with battle.
When he beat with a bone on the platter, those with food licked china bowls   and those who had food feasted greatly, sitting at leisure.
His verses of song were forty, perhaps more   they exceeded four tens and that is correct, for let me not state what is wrong.
By the grace of Allah, take these, take these, for the Shah has come to the dancing   The Shah has come to the dance; arise everyone and let me play.'

When the songs' refrain increased   and the drumming loudly swelled   he was cutting away there   at his handcuffs and chains.
While the clapping increased   he was cutting away quickly until when the clapping stopped   he said to them, Lift up your eyes.
And pausing in their dance   Liyongo appeared   and fear fell upon them   and they were lost in fright as they ran away.
For they all ran away   there was no one left   Liyongo came forth   and returned once again to the mainland . . .

Africa's Plea

by Roland Tombekai Dempster

I am not you —
but you will not
give me a chance,
will not let me be *me*.

'If I were you' —
but you know
I am not you,
yet you will not
let me be *me*.

You meddle, interfere
in my affairs
as if they were yours
and you were me.

You are unfair, unwise,
foolish to think
that I can be you,
talk, act
and think like you.

God made me *me*.
He made you *you*.
Let me be *me*.
For God's sake

Voices of Africa

BARBARA NOLEN, a graduate of Smith College, studied also at Stamford and Radcliffe, and with her husband David Fales Strong has researched and travelled widely in Africa. She has written several other books about African authors.

ABIOSEH NICOL is a poet, diplomat, scientist and political historian. He took his degree at Cambridge University, was Principal of the University College of Sierra Leone, and for three years was his country's ambassador to the United Nations.

Fontana African Novels

More Voices of Africa	*Barbara Nolen (Ed.)*
Danda	*Nkem Nwankwo*
The Radiance of the King	*Camara Laye*
A Dream of Africa	*Camara Laye*
The African Child	*Camara Laye*
The Gab Boys	*Cameron Duodu*
Emperor of the Sea	*Obi B. Egbuna*
The Naked Gods	*Chukwuemeka Ike*
Toads for Supper	*Chukwuemeka Ike*
The Potter's Wheel	*Chukwuemeka Ike*
The Wanderers	*Ezekiel Mphahlele*
The Voice	*Gabriel Okara*
The Interpreters	*Wole Soyinka*